GCSE ENGLISH LITERATURE

Teacher Guide

for OCR

D1806538

Annie Fox
Garrett O'Doherty
Angela Topping
Carmel Waldron

OCR
RECOGNISING ACHIEVEMENT

OXFORD
UNIVERSITY PRESS

Official Publisher Partnership

OXFORD
UNIVERSITY PRESS

Great Clarendon Street, Oxford OX2 6DP

Oxford University Press is a department of the University of Oxford.
It furthers the University's objective of excellence in research,
scholarship, and education by publishing worldwide in

Oxford   New York

Auckland   Cape Town   Dar es Salaam   Hong Kong   Karachi
Kuala Lumpur   Madrid   Melbourne   Mexico City   Nairobi
New Delhi   Shanghai   Taipei   Toronto

With offices in

Argentina   Austria   Brazil   Chile   Czech Republic   France   Greece
Guatemala   Hungary   Italy   Japan   Poland   Portugal   Singapore
South Korea   Switzerland   Thailand   Turkey   Ukraine   Vietnam

Oxford is a registered trade mark of Oxford University Press
in the UK and in certain other countries

© Oxford University Press 2010

The moral rights of the authors have been asserted

Database right Oxford University Press (maker)

First published 2010

British Library Cataloguing in Publication Data

Data available

ISBN 978-0-19-832951-0

10 9 8 7 6 5 4 3 2 1

Printed in Great Britain by Bell and Bain Ltd., Glasgow

Mixed Sources
Product group from well-managed
forests and other controlled sources
www.fsc.org   Cert no. TT-COC-002769
© 1996 Forest Stewardship Council

Contents

GCSE English Literature for OCR offers a comprehensive, endorsed package of classroom-friendly resources fully in line with the 2010 OCR GCSE English Literature specifications. Written by OCR examiners and Teachit contributors, it offers teachers and students at all levels of ability a simple, clear approach to the specification, with full support for Controlled Assessment and exam requirements. All of the materials have been carefully matched to the unit requirements of the OCR GCSE English Literature specification.

Course components

The course consists of the core Student Book (suitable for students at both Foundation and Higher levels), the Access Student Book (suitable for lower level Foundation and Entry Level students), this Teacher Guide, an interactive OxBox CD-ROM and a Skills & Practice book to help students achieve their maximum potential.

The Student Book

- Up-to-date content written specifically to cover the 2010 OCR GCSE English specification and endorsed by OCR.
- Each unit includes clear explanations of how to approach and prepare for the exam or Controlled Assessment.
- Course requirements are covered by fun classroom-friendly content and activities written by Teachit contributors, including special 'Try This!' sections for additional creative work.
- Examiner's tips written by a principal examiner are provided throughout, giving students valuable pointers on how to perform to their best ability.
- Students are encouraged to evaluate their progress through learning checklists based on Assessment Objectives.

- Units conclude with sample exam questions or Controlled Assessment tasks, and sample student responses with examiner's comments, to allow students to better understand what is required of them and identify ways to gain a higher mark.

The OxBox CD-ROM

- Includes many further activities and lesson ideas, including editable worksheets and PowerPoints to supplement the Student Book and Teacher Guide.
- PowerPoints and quizzes for every set text and prescribed poet are included, as well as interactive activities, including some with Record & Playback functionality ideal for speaking and listening work.
- Grids, diagrams and sample questions from the Student Book are provided in editable format.
- Ready-made and customizable course and lesson plans are included; the lesson player helps you arrange and launch the resources you want to use in sequence.
- You can add your own resources, and easy-to-follow guidelines are given.
- The OxBox user management facility allows you to easily import class registers and create user accounts for all your students.

Skills & Practice book

- Structured to match the specifications exactly, so students have a clear idea of what is required of them.
- Guides students through exam question types and Controlled Assessment tasks, ensuring that all necessary skills are covered.
- Includes lots of clear, useful advice.
- Each unit includes a 'Boost your grade' section, ensuring students at all levels are given the opportunity to maximize their potential.

Unit I: Literary Heritage Linked Texts

SECTION	OUTLINE	ASSESSMENT OBJECTIVE	STUDENT BOOK	OTHER RELEVANT COMPONENTS
Shakespeare and Film/ Audio/Live Performance	Controlled Assessment 10%	AO1 • Respond to texts critically and imaginatively. • Select and evaluate relevant textual detail to illustrate and support interpretations. AO3 • Make comparisons and explain links between texts, evaluating writers' different ways of expressing meaning and achieving effects.	Ch 1.1 Responding to a Shakespeare Text Ch 1.2 Links Between Shakespeare and Film	Teacher Guide Chapters 1.1–1.2 OxBox CD-ROM Unit 1 Skills & Practice Book Unit 1
Literary Heritage Poetry	Controlled Assessment 15%	AO1 • Respond to texts critically and imaginatively. • Select and evaluate relevant textual detail to illustrate and support interpretations. AO3 • Make comparisons and explain links between texts, evaluating writers' different ways of expressing meaning and achieving effects.	Ch 1.3 Responding to Poetry Ch 1.4 Explaining the Links Between Poems	Teacher Guide Chapters 1.3–1.4 OxBox CD-ROM Unit 1 Skills & Practice Book Unit 1

Unit 2: Modern Drama

SECTION	OUTLINE	ASSESSMENT OBJECTIVE	STUDENT BOOK	OTHER RELEVANT COMPONENTS
	Exam 25%	AO1 • Respond to texts critically and imaginatively. • Select and evaluate relevant textual detail to illustrate and support interpretations. AO2 • Explain how language, structure and form contribute to writers' presentation of ideas, themes and settings.	Ch 2.1 Passage-Based Questions Ch 2.2 Comment, Criticism and Analysis	Teacher Guide Chapters 2.1–2.2 OxBox CD-ROM Unit 2 Skills & Practice Book Unit 2

Unit 3: Prose from Different Cultures

SECTION	OUTLINE	ASSESSMENT OBJECTIVE	STUDENT BOOK	OTHER RELEVANT COMPONENTS
	Exam 25%	AO2 • Explain how language, structure and form contribute to writers' presentation of ideas, themes and settings. AO4 • Relate texts to their social, cultural and historical contexts. • Explain how texts have been influential and significant to self and other readers in different contexts and at different times.	Ch 3.1 Passage-Based Questions Ch 3.2 Comment, Criticism and Analysis	Teacher Guide Chapters 3.1–3.2 OxBox CD-ROM Unit 3 Skills & Practice Book Unit 3

Unit 4: Literary Heritage Prose and Contemporary Poetry

SECTION	OUTLINE	ASSESSMENT OBJECTIVE	STUDENT BOOK	OTHER RELEVANT COMPONENTS
Literary Heritage Prose	Exam 15%	AO1 • Respond to texts critically and imaginatively. • Select and evaluate relevant textual detail to illustrate and support interpretations. AO2 • Explain how language, structure and form contribute to writers' presentation of ideas, themes and settings.	Ch 4.1 Passage-Based Questions Chapter 4.2 Comment, Criticism and Analysis	Teacher Guide Chapters 1.1–1.2 OxBox CD-ROM Unit 1 Skills & Practice Book Unit 1
Contemporary Poetry	Exam 10%	AO1 • Respond to texts critically and imaginatively. • Select and evaluate relevant textual detail to illustrate and support interpretations. AO2 • Explain how language, structure and form contribute to writers' presentation of ideas, themes and settings.	Ch 4.3 Anthology: Reading Poetry Ch 4.4 Anthology: Analysing Poetry Ch 4.5 Unseen poetry	Teacher Guide Chapters 4.3–4.5 OxBox CD-ROM Unit 1 Skills & Practice Book Unit 1

Unit 1

Literary Heritage Linked Texts

What you need to know

Unit 1 is assessed through Controlled Assessment. Like the other three units of GCSE English Literature, it counts for 25% of the total GCSE mark. However, unlike the examined units, it is not split into Foundation and Higher tiers.

Unit 1 is divided into two areas of study:

- **Shakespeare and Film/Audio/Live Performance (10%)**
  Students answer one question on the Shakespeare text studied linked to a film, audio or live performance of the play. This task will require comment, criticism and analysis of aspects of the selected play and of linked scenes from the chosen film or audio version.

  Plays set for study are: *Julius Caesar*, *The Merchant of Venice*, *Macbeth* and *Romeo & Juliet*.

- **Literary Heritage Poetry (15%)**
  Students study one poet from a choice of six and complete one comparative task linking two poems they have studied.

  Students study fifteen poems by ONE of the following poets: *Robert Browning*, *Thomas Hardy*, *Wilfred Owen*, *Christina Rossetti* and *William Shakespeare (sonnets)* or they can choose to study *The General Prologue to the Canterbury Tales* by Geoffrey Chaucer. All poetry is included in the OCR Anthology, *Reflections*.

All tasks are set by OCR, and will be made available from June of every year to allow time for planning. Tasks can be completed at any point in the academic year, provided they meet the deadline for submission.

The stages of Controlled Assessment

Completing the Controlled Assessment takes place in a series of four stages:

1. Introduction to the task
1-2 hours

A teacher-led introduction to the Controlled Assessment tasks.

2. Preparation
16-20 hours

This stage covers the normal teaching of the relevant texts and can include group work. You will be able to give students support and guidance during this stage, including explaining the task, advising on how it might be approached, advising on resources and ensuring candidates are aware of key elements that should be included in their final pieces.

3. Research
4–6 hours
Students are allowed to undertake research using available resources both in and outside of the classroom and may also work with other students as necessary. Any research materials and references will need to be acknowledged appropriately in their final submissions.

4. Evaluation
3 hours per task
Students produce their two pieces of work under controlled conditions. They will be allowed to bring the following in with them:

- notes (there is no restriction on the number of pages, but notes must not form a draft response; OCR recommends that notes be submitted along with students' final responses)
- clean, un-annotated copies of texts, dictionaries and thesauri. The tasks may be word processed but email and Internet access must be switched off.

Each task should take up to three hours and be up to 1,000 words. The allocated time may be split into more than one session as you see fit, but work must be collected and stored securely between sessions. No teacher feedback is allowed during the evaluation phase.

Assessment Objectives
The Assessment Objectives covered in this unit are:

AO1
Respond to texts critically and imaginatively; select and evaluate relevant textual detail to illustrate and support interpretations.

AO3
Make comparisons and explain links between texts, evaluating writers' different ways of expressing meaning and achieving effects.

1.1 Responding to a Shakespeare Text

Assessment Objectives

AO1

- Respond to texts critically and imaginatively.

- Select and evaluate relevant textual detail to illustrate and support interpretations.

Ideas for starters

- Working in pairs, ask the students to record what they know about Shakespeare's life and plays, then feed back to create a whole class spider diagram of Shakespeare facts.
- Show the class pictures of the Globe theatre and a modern theatre and ask them to discuss the differences between them, including architecture, lighting and where the audience is positioned. How do they think going to a theatre in Shakespeare's time would be different from going to the theatre today?
- Have the students create an acrostic poem from the name 'Shakespeare' to convey their knowledge about his plays.
- On sticky notes, ask the students to record any questions they have about Shakespeare. Collect them in and read them out at the end of the lesson, seeing how many the class can now answer.
- Use **Interactives 1.1.1** and **1.1.2** to teach students the features of dramas and comedies.

Why is Shakespeare still studied and performed?

Key ideas
- Although he died in 1616, Shakespeare's plays are still performed and studied throughout the world.

ACTIVITY 1    tweakit

How does it work?
Students read four opinions about the value of studying Shakespeare and evaluate them. They then use the statements as prompts to develop a short piece of writing expressing their own knowledge and opinions on studying Shakespeare.

Try this!
Working in small groups, students discuss the statements and then rank them from 1 to 4 in order of agreement. Take feedback from the whole class.

Or this!

Students each take one of the statements and create a one minute speech developing the point of view expressed in that statement, supported by evidence from their own experiences of studying Shakespeare.

What is interpretation?

Key ideas

- An interpretation is a point of view about the meaning and intention of a text.
- Shakespeare's plays are open to different interpretations, including themes, setting and casting.

Stagecraft: how to analyse a play

Key ideas

- Plays are set out differently to other texts. Features include: characters, dialogue and stage directions.
- Shakespeare's plays can be divided into comedies and tragedies and each has specific features.

ACTIVITY 2    **tweakit**

How does it work?

Students read about the conventions of Shakespearean comedies and tragedies and then apply this knowledge to the play they are studying by creating a spider diagram identifying the comic and/or tragic elements in the play. They will also consider that there can be comic elements in a tragedy or tragic elements in a comedy.

Try this!

Label one corner of the classroom 'Tragedy' and the opposite corner 'Comedy'. Ask the students to move to the area of the room which best describes the play they are studying or to stay in the middle if they think it is a mixture. Ask individuals in different parts of the room to explain why they think the play is comic, tragic or a combination.

Or this! (for a mixed ability class)

Assign groups different aspects of the play to analyse (characters, events, setting and ending) using the spider diagram on **Activity Sheet 1.1.1** and then feed back their opinions on the comic and tragic elements to the whole class.

Or this! (for a mixed ability class)

Have the students produce a detailed poster illustrating the comic or tragic elements of the play they are studying. Encourage them to use striking visual images so that it will make a helpful, attractive wall display.

Characterization: Lady Macbeth/Shylock

Key ideas

- Lady Macbeth would have originally been played by a boy, but is now one of the most important female Shakespearean roles.
- Shylock is one of Shakespeare's most controversial characters. He could be sympathetic, frightening or amusing.

ACTIVITY 3
 tweakit

How does it work?

Students read a short excerpt from *Macbeth* and consider how actors might interpret the roles through facial expressions, tone of voice and body language. They will also consider the specific meaning of certain lines and what they tell us about the relationship between the two characters.

Try this!

Have the students read the extract in pairs and experiment with different readings and interpretations, such as Lady Macbeth being very domineering or sly or persuasive. **Record & Playback 1.1.1** can be used to help them reflect on their experiments.

Or this! (for mixed ability groups)

Have pairs perform their interpretations to the class, with another student appointed to 'direct' the scene. The class can then vote for the group whose interpretation is closest to how they imagine the scene should be performed.

Or this! (for less confident students)

Two students read the lines, while another two convey the body language and facial expressions of the characters.

ACTIVITY 4
 tweakit

How does it work?

Students complete a close character study of Shylock, first by answering the questions in the margins of the annotated passage, then by reading and making notes on the rest of Act 1, Scene 3. They should find textual evidence to support their view of the character of Shylock.

Try this!

In pairs, have students experiment with one of two interpretations of Shylock: either he is a sympathetic but cautious businessman or he is a villain craftily planning revenge on Antonio. Have them discuss what other interpretations they might try and which they feel works best with the text.

Or this!

Students create a storyboard showing how they would stage key moments from Act 1, Scene 3.

Or this! (for less confident students)

Ask students to improvise a modern scene in which someone is asking for a loan. Discuss how this is similar to or different from the request Bassanio is making.

Themes: love in Romeo & Juliet/ambition in Macbeth

Key ideas

- A theme is a significant topic or idea that is developed in a text.
- Students should look at themes in relation to language and characters, and can connect the play's theme with its message.
- The most apparent theme in *Romeo & Juliet* is love; many different types of love are explored in the play.
- Macbeth's tragic flaw is ambition.

ACTIVITY 5  **tweakit**

How does it work?

The theme of love in *Romeo & Juliet* is explored. Students consider the different types of love in the play by completing a grid with a selection of quotations from the play, which they must explain, as well as identifying the kind of love the line exemplifies.

Try this!

Working in pairs, have each student take it in turns to locate the quotations in the play, while the other writes an explanation of the quotation onto **Activity Sheet 1.1.2**.

Or this! (for higher ability)

Have students find a further five quotations about love from the play and explain what impression the language used in the quotations gives about the characters' attitudes to love. Ask them to identify any imagery used.

Or this! (for lower ability)

Students could create visual images to demonstrate the different types of love and write the quotations under the images.

ACTIVITY 6  **tweakit**

How does it work?

Students create their own 'Love' chart for the play they are studying (**Activity Sheet 1.1.3**). They should identify the types of love in their play (for example: parental love, love of money, self love, love of country, romantic love) and find quotations from the play about each. They should then explain what the line tells them about how this type of love is presented.

Try this! (for higher ability)

Have the students work in pairs to locate quotations. Set more able students the challenge of finding twice as many quotations.

Or this!

Create a whole-class chart, either on an A2 piece of paper or on your interactive whiteboard, to which students can contribute as they read the play.

ACTIVITY 7  tweakit

How does it work?

In order to explore the theme of ambition in *Macbeth*, students complete a spider diagram (**Activity Sheet 1.1.4**), looking particularly at the sources of Macbeth's ambition; what he does because of it and the price he ultimately pays for it. Those studying *Julius Caesar* could create a similar spider diagram on the theme of ambition. They then write a paragraph about ambition in the play, supporting their ideas with quotations from the text.

Try this!

Divide the class into thirds and ask each third to look at one aspect of ambition (source, actions or price). Ask each group to find at least three quotations about the aspect of ambition they are exploring and to explain what it tells us about this theme.

Or this!

Write on the board: *Is ambition always wrong?* Ask the class to debate the positive and negative aspects of ambition.

Or this!

Students 'buddy assess' each other's paragraphs, giving up to two marks for each of the following: points about source of ambition; points about actions caused by ambition; points about price of ambition; use of quotation; accuracy and clarity of writing.

ACTIVITY 8  tweakit

How does it work?

Students explore other themes in the play they are studying and make a PowerPoint presentation showing how the theme is developed in the play. They must support their ideas with quotations from the play.

Try this!

Start the lesson with the whole class listing as many themes as they can find in the play they are studying. Then, working in small groups, they create a poster based on one of the themes.

Or this! (for higher ability)

Encourage students to look at symbolism and how Shakespeare uses it when representing themes such as fate.

Or this! (for mixed ability groups)

Have students work in groups to prepare their PowerPoint presentations. They may divide duties, with some being responsible for finding quotations, others for finding or creating the visual images and others for writing the script. Encourage them to make the displays entertaining, informative and memorable.

Language: revealing characters' emotions

Key ideas

- Shakespeare's vivid use of language is renowned.
- Shakespeare's plays are written in verse and prose, using techniques like rhyme, metaphor and alliteration.
- This language can be used to reveal characters' psychological state.

ACTIVITY 9

 tweakit

How does it work?

Focusing on language, the students closely read and compare two short excerpts in which the language used reveals the psychological states of the characters. Using the questions in the margins, the students then compare how the language in each piece reveals the characters' states of mind.

Try this!

Ask students to work in pairs underlining the key words and phrases in each passage that they believe an actor should emphasize in his or her delivery.

Or this!

Play an audio version of the speeches to the class and ask them to note the words and phrases that the actors emphasize and how they do this (speaking more slowly, changing their pitch, increasing their volume, etc.). What do they learn about the characters from the choices the actors make?

Or this! (for less confident writers)

Ask the class to contribute a list of comparative words and phrases that they could use in their written passage, such as 'in contrast', 'similarly', 'both' and 'unlike'. Encourage students to use short embedded quotations from these passages when making their comparisons.

Supporting your interpretation of the play

Key ideas

- Students must show they respond personally and offer their own interpretations.
- Students must use relevant details from the play to support their ideas.
- Planning time should include finding quotations and ordering ideas.

How does it work?

Focusing on a key scene from the play they are studying, students complete a grid analysing and offering a directorial interpretation of that scene (**Activity Sheet 1.1.5**). They are encouraged to read the scene carefully, locate evidence from the text and explain the effect of the quotations they select.

Try this!

Choose two key scenes for students to analyse, having half the class working on one scene and the rest on the other. Ask for a presentation on each scene and invite the rest of the class to add in more details or ideas.

Or this!

Ask students to use the ideas and evidence from the grid to answer an essay question explaining the importance of their chosen scene to the key themes of the play they are studying.

Or this!

Have the class imagine that they have been asked to make a 'pitch' to direct a production of their play. Using the evidence from their chart, they should present their concept for the play. The class can vote on who 'gets the job'.

Ideas for plenaries

- Have a student face the class with his or her back to the whiteboard, while you write the name of a character (Shylock, Lady Macbeth, the Nurse, etc.) over his or her head on the board for the class to see. The student must ask the class up to ten questions, that require a 'yes' or 'no' answer, to try to determine which character he or she is.

- Play 'Just a Minute': ask students to speak for a minute, without hesitation, deviation or repetition, about a theme or a character from the play they are studying.

- Return to the original spider diagram or questions about Shakespeare (see Starters) and ask them to fill in any new information they now have.

- Invite up to three students to give a 'mini-teach' summary of what was learned in that day's lesson, concluding with a quick-fire quiz.

Assessment Objectives

AO1

- Respond to texts critically and imaginatively.

- Select and evaluate relevant textual detail to illustrate and support interpretations.

AO3

- Make comparisons and explain links between texts, evaluating writers' different ways of expressing meaning and achieving effects.

Ideas for starters

- Ask the students to explain in more than a hundred words what their favourite film is and why.
- Present the class with a series of stills from films and ask them to select which are based on Shakespeare plays. How did they come to this conclusion?
- 'Who said that?': Have a small pile of quotations from different characters from the play written on slips of paper. Working in pairs, students sort them into which character said the line. (There should be one quotation per character.) Bonus points can be given if they are also in the correct sequence of when the line is said in the play. Extra bonus points can be given for the most dramatic and entertaining reading of one of the lines.
- Ask the class to prepare a one minute speech agreeing or disagreeing with the statement: 'Going to see films is better than going to the theatre.'

Why film Shakespeare's plays?

Key ideas
- Shakespeare has provided inspiration for cinema since the early days of film.
- Film versions can give people who don't go to the theatre the opportunity to experience Shakespeare's work.

ACTIVITY 1    tweakit

How does it work?
Working with a partner, students read through a series of statements and decide which apply to theatre performances, which to films and which can be applied to both.

Try this!

Ask students to discuss each statement and to try to think of specific examples to support their ideas. For example, can they think of famous actors whom they have seen in a Shakespearean film? Have they ever seen a live performance of a play by Shakespeare?

Or this! (for less confident students)

Invite students to reflect on their own movie-going experiences. Ask them to list which of the following made their favourite films appealing: famous actors; realistic acting; special effects; script; or visual images. Ask them to give short examples.

Or this!

The activity can also be completed using **Interactive 1.2.1**, a quiz on the differences between stage and screen.

ACTIVITY 2  **tweakit**

How does it work?

Students are introduced to the term 'naturalism' and use it in a discussion about the challenges of filming Shakespeare's plays.

Try this!

Students work in pairs on a short speech or scene from the play they are studying. Ask them to attempt to perform the speech in a naturalistic way and then in a heightened, stylized (possibly over-the-top) way. Which style do they associate more with film acting? Can either style be used in films?

Or this! (for higher ability)

Ask the students to imagine they have been commissioned to direct a short film based on the play that they are studying which would appeal to teenagers. Would they make it naturalistic or not? Ask them to write a short letter to a producer explaining how they would handle Shakespeare's language and ideas in the film.

Using film techniques to convey meaning

Key ideas

• The director of a film must make a number of key decisions, for example, what to cut, film techniques, setting, casting.

ACTIVITY 3  **tweakit**

How does it work?

The students learn the definitions for key filmmaking techniques and then complete a grid suggesting how these techniques could be used when filming a film based on a Shakespeare play.

Try this!

Show the class a short sequence from the film they are studying and ask them to use the chart (**Activity Sheet 1.2.1**) to note any of the techniques used. At the bottom of the chart they can use spare boxes to note other techniques they spot, such as montage or flashback.

Or this!

Have students create a storyboard to accompany a short sequence from the play they are studying. Ask them to indicate on the storyboard any techniques they would use, such as camera angles and voiceover. They can then compare their ideas with an actual film of the play.

Modernizing Shakespeare: Romeo + Juliet

Key ideas

- Baz Luhrmann's *Romeo + Juliet* was a successful example of a modernized film version and introduced the play to a new audience.

ACTIVITY 4  **tweakit**

How does it work?

In order to analyse the qualities needed to portray a given character, students work in pairs to prepare a casting brief for the lead characters in the play they are studying.

Try this!

Ask students to prepare a detailed description of the type of actor needed to portray a character they are studying. Encourage them to look for clues in the text about the character's age, emotions and appearance. They may also visit websites, such as that of the Royal Shakespeare Company (www.rsc.org.uk/explore), to research previous casting of these roles.

Or this! (for lower ability)

Provide visual prompts for the type of actors students might consider to play these roles. Encourage them to use visual images from the Internet or magazines, to produce a casting advertisement which can then be used as a wall display to remind them of the various characters.

ACTIVITY 5  **tweakit**

How does it work?

Students watch the balcony scene (Act 2, Scene 2) from the film *Romeo + Juliet*. They then analyse it by answering three questions about design and directorial choices. (**Activity Sheet 1.2.2** can be used for this.)

Try this!

Divide the class into thirds and have one third focusing on how the scene has been updated; one on the set and costumes; and one on the creation of suspense and danger. Then have each group feed back to the class.

Or this! (for higher ability)

Make a copy of Act 2, Scene 2 and have students annotate the text to show how it was filmed; for example, edits, close-ups, camera angles and soundtrack. Ask them to discuss how these choices will affect an audience's understanding of this scene.

Or this! (for a mixed ability group)

Reinforce the students' understanding of media terminology by asking them to write a paragraph about how this scene was filmed using media terms such as 'editing', 'soundtrack', 'close-up', 'high angle shot', etc.

Acting Shakespeare for film

Key ideas

- A number of different interpretations of character are possible for different actors from the same script.
- Techniques actors use include: vocal skills, facial expressions and body language.

ACTIVITY 6    **tweakit**

How does it work?

Students watch Act 1, Scene 3 from *The Merchant of Venice* in two contrasting film versions, then complete a grid comparing the two portrayals of Shylock.

Try this!

Let students work on their own to complete the grid (**Activity Sheet 1.2.3**). Then put them in pairs or small groups to add more detailed observations and to consider each others' opinions about the performances. Afterwards, conduct a whole class discussion about which portrayal they preferred and why.

Or this! (for students who need a challenge)

Have the students try to recreate a small section of each of the filmed performances, including facial expressions, body language and vocal skills. Ask the class to note when the performers have varied their performance from that of the actor in the film and how this affects the impact of their performance.

Or this! (for less confident students)

Ask the students in groups to recreate a series of four or five 'freeze frames' from the film and to note aspects of the performances such as stance, proximity and facial expression.

Films and filmed stage productions

Key ideas

- Some film versions of Shakespeare begin as stage productions. Directors must decide how closely the film will resemble the theatrical production.
- For example, the Trevor Nunn version of *Macbeth* is based on a stage production and uses costumes, props and sets from this. The Roman Polanski film version is not based on a stage production and is a highly filmic production.

ACTIVITY 7  tweakit

How does it work?

Students read an extract from Act 2, Scene 2 of *Macbeth* and answer detailed questions about how the scene could be interpreted. They then watch two versions of the scene: Trevor Nunn's 1979 version and Roman Polanski's 1971 film, and complete a comparison grid (**Activity Sheet 1.2.4**). As an extension task, they are invited to watch Akira Kurosawa's *Throne of Blood*.

Try this!

Students watch the filmed scenes several times. They should not make notes the first time, but just take in the two interpretations. The second time they watch the scene, ask them to work in pairs and have one person focus more on the performance of Lady Macbeth and the other on Macbeth. Invite them to share their notes about the characters with each other.

Or this! (for lower ability)

Provide the students with a photocopy of the scene with key lines highlighted and ask them to make notes or drawings on the text showing what the actors are doing at those specific points in the scene.

Or this! (for higher ability)

Show a section of the Akira Kurosawa film *Throne of Blood* and ask students to add in a column on their chart comparing that film with the other two.

Identifying with characters

Key ideas

- An interpretation of a play includes how sympathetic certain characters are. For example, the character of Shylock is widely debated and open to a number of interpretations.
- Students will be required to make connections between Shakespeare's written work and one or more film, audio or stage versions.

- Students will analyse what Shakespeare wrote and how these scenes were interpreted.
- They will need to select relevant quotations to support their ideas.

ACTIVITY 8

 **tweakit**

How does it work?

Using evidence from three key scenes, students debate whether or not Shylock is a villain or a victim. They read the scenes, noting significant lines about how Shylock is portrayed, watch at least one filmed performance and prepare a two minute speech promoting their point of view of Shylock.

Try this!

In order to get a more exciting debate, you may need to assign certain sides of the argument to specific students. Ideally, you should have an equal number arguing for Shylock being a villain as for him being a victim, so you will need to explain that in this debating exercise, it is the quality of the reasoning and expression that is important, rather than the individual point of view. Students can record their debate using **Record & Playback 1.2.1** and use this to facilitate self or peer review.

Or this! (for less confident students)

Hand out a list of 'argument' words and phrases to support the preparation of the speeches, such as 'In my opinion', 'I strongly disagree', 'For example', 'Looking at the evidence', etc.

ACTIVITY 9

 **tweakit**

How does it work?

Students create a flow diagram to track the development of a character. In this instance they are looking for positive and/or negative comments made by or about Shylock, in order to reach an opinion about whether or not he is a villain.

Try this!

Hand out copies of **Activity Sheet 1.2.5** for students to use. Suggest that they colour code the quotations so that it is clear if they have found positive or negative evidence.

Or this! (for higher ability)

The flow chart can be adapted to track the progress of another character in *The Merchant of Venice* or one of the other Shakespeare texts. Suggest that more able students select another character and locate evidence of that character's progression in three key scenes. Possible characters to track include Portia, Romeo, Lady Macbeth or Mark Antony. Encourage the students to look for turning points.

ACTIVITY 10    **tweakit**

How does it work?

Students read a sample essay question and a selection of quotations from the Prologue and Act 1, Scene 1 of *Romeo & Juliet*. They examine the language of the quotations and use them to answer the essay question.

Try this!

Have the students make a grid to help them analyse the quotations. They should note who says the line, what the context is and any particular language features (oxymorons, hyperbole, repetition, imagery). Encourage them to make a detailed plan which includes language analysis before beginning to write their essay.

Or this! (for lower ability)

Have students work in groups of three and assign each group one of the lines. One student is responsible for performing the line, one identifies who said the line and the third explains what the line means. Each group performs their line and shares their ideas with the class, then students can complete their grids individually.

ACTIVITY 11    **tweakit**

How does it work?

Students read two brief sample student responses about the opening of *The Merchant of Venice*. They highlight details from the essays and suggest ways in which the essays could be improved and completed. Copies of the student responses can be found on **Activity Sheet 1.2.6**.

Try this!

Remind the students of the assessment criteria for this unit (on page 7 of the Student Book) and ask them to explain what AO1 and AO3 mean in their own words. Then return to the student responses and ask them to indicate when a point meets one of the Assessment Objectives.

Or this!

Ask students to write improved versions of these responses (or a similar assignment on the scene(s)/play they are studying) and then ask them to 'buddy assess' each other's work out of a possible total of 10. They should give one mark for each quotation used well (up to three marks); up to three marks for their analysis of the interpretation of the scene(s); up to three marks for any comparisons they make and one mark for the quality and accuracy of the writing.

Try This!

Teaching notes

- Use the students' knowledge of media to increase their understanding of interpretation. Ask them to consider carefully what effects they hope to achieve and how they could achieve them through media techniques like the use of a soundtrack and quick editing.

- Try modelling an example of a storyboard, stressing to students that you do not have to be a good artist to draw an interesting storyboard. Ask them to avoid stick figures, as they need to show if something is being shot in close-up, mid-shot or long-shot. Encourage them to imagine exactly what will fill the frame.

- Mixed and low ability groups find it helpful to experiment with using 'modern' language, in order to make sure they fully understand the scene. However, remind them they will have to write about Shakespeare's original language.

- Activity 4: More able students may succeed in the 'talk show host' role, making sure that the show has pace and interest. This task can be adapted to serve as a Speaking and Listening exercise.

Ideas for plenaries

- 'You say/We pay' (or 'What Media Term Am I?'): Have a student stand in front of the whiteboard. Write a media term over his or her head (close-up, montage, voiceover, etc.) and ask another student to describe what the term means without using the actual word (or any part of it). 'Pay' points to teams who get the description and answer right.

- Return to Activity 1 on page 16 and ask the students if, after studying the Shakespeare films, they still have the same opinions about theatre versus films. Ask them to give specific examples from the film(s) they are studying.

- Shakespeare Charades: A student mimes a significant line from the play and whoever is able to recite the line correctly wins.

- Have the class exchange and assess examples of their written work. Ask the student 'assessors' to highlight at least one strong point or sentence from the work they are reading and suggest one target for improvement. Create a list for the whole class of the strong points and targets for improvement. Have each student write down at least one target for improvement that applies to him or her.

Assessment Objectives

AO1

- Respond to texts critically and imaginatively.

- Select and evaluate relevant textual detail to illustrate and support interpretations.

Ideas for starters

- Divide the class into three groups. Two of these come up with nouns, one with adjectives. Taking each group in turn, create random similes by adding 'as' in between the nouns and adjectives to form a simile; for example, *a banana as scary as a dustbin*. Results can be hilarious!

- Write several simple colour words such as 'blue', 'green' and 'red' on the board. Give students three minutes to think of some other words for these colours. Collect these from the class and discuss them. They should come up with examples like: (for red) *scarlet, crimson, puce, rose, maroon, strawberry, burgundy, ruby, cherry*. Then try the words out in different sentences, such as: *The girl wore _____ lipstick*. What effect does each different colour word have? Consider connotations; for example scarlet woman. Further colour examples could be: (blue) *indigo, sky, lapis, navy, cerulean, sapphire, azure*; (green) *vermilion, emerald, jade, olive*.

- Introduce spider diagrams as a way of representing information visually (page 32). To kick them off, have students create a quick diagram about themselves and their hobbies.

Why poets use literary devices

Key ideas

- Literary devices allow poets to communicate effectively with the reader. Words and phrases are carefully selected to prompt specific emotions and create effects in the reader.

- In studying poetry, students must think carefully about what literary devices are used and why, and what effects they create.

ACTIVITY 1
 tweakit

How does it work?
Students use a diagram to remind them of different literary devices. Terms could be grouped into categories such as comparisons, imagery, sound or form.

Try this! (for lower ability)

Show the class some examples of spider diagrams and demonstrate how to create these. They can then use **Activity Sheet 1.3.1** to complete their spider diagrams.

Or this!

Ask students to suggest other ways of representing information visually, such as a tree, or a washing line, or a garden of different plants. The only limit is their imagination.

Or this!

Ask different groups of students to create posters of the different sections of the spider diagram for classroom display.

Responding with insight and imagination

Key ideas

- Insight means having ideas of your own about a poem.
- The best way to explore these ideas is to annotate the poem.
- Students must refer closely to the text with short quotations in context when writing about poems.

ACTIVITY 2

How does it work?

Students work in pairs or groups to choose a poem and annotate it (using the work on 'Exposure' on page 34 as a model) to help them explore the poem independently. They then write a paragraph on one stanza of their poem.

Try this!

Each group or pair reports back to the class by reading their chosen poem and explaining their annotations.

Or this! (if you have an interactive whiteboard)

Students add their annotations to a copy on the whiteboard so the rest of the class can add those they agree with more easily.

ACTIVITY 3

How does it work?

Students compare the final version of 'Anthem for Doomed Youth' with Wilfred Owen's draft.

Try this!

Students substitute the words and phrases in the final draft for the ones Owen originally considered to examine the effect of the changes.

Or this!

Give the class a copy of the final version and a version using the phrases from the drafts and see which they think is the finished one. Ask them for their reasons. Take a class vote before revealing which one was ultimately published.

Poetry by design

Key ideas

- Poets create an overall structure and shape for their poems – some unique, some well-established.
- A sonnet is a traditional poetic form, using 14 lines of iambic pentameter and including a turn.
- In Shakespearean sonnets the turn comes after 12 lines.
- A quatrain is a set of four lines.

ACTIVITY 4  **tweakit**

How does it work?

Students look at the structure of two Shakespeare sonnets. (This can be done whether or not he is their set poet. They can then apply their knowledge to poems they are studying in Activity 5.)

Try this!

Introduce the poem by asking the class to think of corny chat-up lines they have heard. Write examples on the board.

Or this!

Give students the first 12 lines, then ask them to think what could be said to get the girlfriend back after upsetting her. Reveal how Shakespeare does it in the final two lines.

Or this!

Use the linking activity in **Interactive 1.3.1** to teach the different literary terms associated with sonnets.

ACTIVITY 5  **tweakit**

How does it work?

Students apply the understanding of structure they gained from Activity 4 to two or three poems by their chosen poet.

Try this!

Give small groups of students cut up photocopies of the poems they are studying, with the stanzas or lines separated. Ask them to arrange them in the order they think works, then present their version to the class with their reasons. Compare their version to the original poems to discover the reasons for the poets' choices.

Or this!

Give small groups of students different coloured highlighter pens and enlarged copies of their poems. Ask them to mark where they think the poem moves on to a different point, and then number the points. They should consider why the poet has placed the points in that order.

People in poetry

Key ideas

• Geoffrey Chaucer wrote *The Canterbury Tales* in Middle English about a group of pilgrims.

ACTIVITY 6

How does it work?

Students create a dating profile for Chaucer's squire.

Try this!

Students look at a model of a suitable Internet dating profile on a print out, or pool their knowledge of what might be included in a profile. They work together in groups or pairs to produce the squire's profile. This could be word-processed and include clipart, for an authentic look.

Or this!

As an extension task, students work in expert groups to prepare profiles for other characters from the Prologue. These would make an interesting classroom display.

ACTIVITY 7

How does it work?

Using the work done in Activity 6, students role-play a speed dating scenario for Chaucer's characters from the Prologue. Each expert group devises some questions they think their character would ask or be asked so that a speed dating session can be simulated.

Try this!

Students make a name card for the character they are representing. Half the students remain at their desks with name cards displayed, while the other half move around the room on the teacher's signal every 10 minutes. Students should not interview another student representing their character. At the end of the session, who would they want to date? And who would they avoid like the plague?

Or this!

Fishbowl (i.e. let the class watch) a few of the interviews, if any of the pairs are willing to redo theirs in front of the class.

Emotions in poetry

Key ideas

• Poets often express their emotions through imagery.

ACTIVITY 8  tweakit

How does it work?
Students work through the guided annotation and exploratory questions on 'The Darkling Thrush' in order to discover how Thomas Hardy expresses his sadness and how the thrush comforts him.

Try this!
Students complete the task using **Activity Sheet 1.3.2** and feed their ideas back to the class by annotating their poem on the interactive whiteboard (IWB).

Or this! (for higher ability)
While the other students are doing the set tasks, the most able prepare similar tasks with answers on the rest of the Hardy poems being studied. They lead a short teaching session with back-up from the class teacher. This could double as a Speaking and Listening task for these pupils.

ACTIVITY 9  tweakit

How does it work?
Students look at 'Promises Like Piecrust', first brainstorming links between piecrust (pastry) and promises (this could include the fact that they begin with the same letter) and then writing a prose version of the poem as a letter to the friend (this should be in modern English).

Try this!
The brainstorm activity would work well as a starter. Use the letter writing task to teach letter writing skills as well as poetry response skills.

Or this! (for higher ability)
While the other students are doing the set tasks, the most able prepare similar tasks, and answers, on the rest of the Rossetti poems being studied. They lead a short teaching session with back-up from the class teacher. This could double as a Speaking and Listening task for these pupils.

ACTIVITY 10  tweakit

How does it work?
Students look at 'Home-Thoughts, from Abroad' to examine Robert Browning's feelings of homesickness. They make a mind-map of spring in England, using the poem as a source and then use these details to write a postcard.

Try this!
Students make an actual postcard, with a suitable image on the front. Each postcard could then be 'sent' to another student in the class.

Or this! (for higher ability)
While the other students are doing the set tasks, the most able prepare

similar tasks, with answers, on the rest of the Browning poems being studied. They lead a short teaching session with back-up from the class teacher. This could double as a Speaking and Listening task for these pupils.

Irony and unreliable narrators

Key ideas

- Irony is when the surface meaning of what is said is different to the underlying meaning and the reader is aware of this difference (for example, Robert Browning's 'My Last Duchess').
- Some poets use a narrator. Some of these are unreliable (the reader cannot trust what they say), for example, Robert Browning's 'Porphyria's Lover'.

ACTIVITY 11

How does it work?

Students analyse 'My Last Duchess' for clues as to whether or not the duke has had his wife killed. They then create a report from the ambassador to the Duke giving reasons against the proposed marriage.

Try this! (for mixed ability groups)

Students work through the guided annotation task in pairs (using **Activity Sheet 1.3.3**) to help them understand how the irony works.

Or this!

Students assemble the clues they have found and set up a murder enquiry, creating a display like those used on crime TV programmes to state the crime and clues, with photographs, etc.

Or this! (for Speaking and Listening work)

Although Activity 11b is set out as a writing task, it could also be used as a role-play task for Speaking and Listening.

ACTIVITY 12

How does it work?

Students revisit the poem 'Porphyria's Lover' to find evidence to use in a piece of writing (newspaper article) or oral work (role-play the trial).

Try this!

Students could split into groups to make a short film about the trial, or put together items for a TV news show, also to be filmed. The films could be uploaded onto the school website as a revision aid.

Or this!

Alternatively, students could write a tabloid article about the story, using a sensational headline and illustrating their article appropriately.

Layers of meaning

Key ideas

- Poetry has different layers of meaning: literal meaning and meaning implied through choice of words, description, and imagery.
- Students should use the text to back up their interpretation.

ACTIVITY 13

 **tweakit**

How does it work?

Students explore the structure and meaning of Thomas Hardy's 'During Wind and Rain' through visual representations such as sketches.

Try this!

Instead of sketches, students could use photographs, or find suitable images on the Internet to illustrate the four 'snapshots'. These could be turned into posters for the classroom or PowerPoint presentations.

Or this! (for media savvy students)

'During Wind and Rain' is ideal for making into a short film using one of the moviemaker packages. Lines from the stanzas should be used as captions or voiceovers.

Or this!

Students could also use drama to create freeze frames using a line from each stanza as a caption.

ACTIVITY 14

 **tweakit**

How does it work?

Students read Thomas Hardy's 'The Ruined Maid' and explore the poem using role-play to explore how Hardy is criticizing society.

Record & Playback 1.3.2 can be used to support this activity.

Try this! (for further Speaking and Listening development)

After the role-play, develop ideas further by hot-seating the two girls and allowing the rest of the class to ask them questions in character.

Or this!

Students draw up a comparison chart contrasting Amelia's life now and the life of the village girl, then discuss who they would rather be.

Ideas for plenaries

- After teaching 'Exposure' by Wilfred Owen (page 33), ask students to choose four phrases from the poem to send home as a postcard to their family. They can add other words. Share the results.
- Hot-seat either the Duke or Porphyria's Lover from the Browning poems. The teacher or a volunteer student can play the character.
- After teaching Sonnet 73 (page 35), ask students to draw a four frame cartoon strip depicting the imagery in each quatrain and the final couplet.

Assessment Objectives

AO3

- Make comparisons and explain links between texts, evaluating writers' different ways of expressing meaning and achieving effects.

Ideas for starters

- Students write down a nursery rhyme they remember without showing anyone. They then partner another student and try to find links between their rhymes. The teacher can have a nursery rhyme ready for projection and show how certain features are common to all nursery rhymes.
- In pairs or small groups, students take one poem each and highlight references to the five senses. They discuss briefly how these create images and mood in the poem, annotating the copies.
- Students work in small groups to take one poem each and write a summary of it in just 50 words.

Looking for similarities and differences

Key ideas

- For the Controlled Assessment, students must identify and discuss similarities and differences between poems. (**Presentation 1.4.1** can be used to introduce students to this section.)
- They should consider such factors as: characters, feelings, situations, language.

Poems linked by theme

Key ideas

- Wilfred Owen's poems are linked by the theme of 'war and the pity of war'.

ACTIVITY 1    tweakit

---

How does it work?

Students identify words and phrases that show physical and mental suffering of soldiers and then complete an empathy exercise.

Try this!

Students can complete Activity 1a and 1b using **Activity Sheet 1.4.1**. For Activity 1c, they can work in pairs to perform their written conversation and record it using **Record & Playback 1.4.1**.

UNIT 1

Or this! (for lower ability)

Phrases describing physical and mental suffering are put on to cards. Students sort them into relevant piles under poem titles and compare them with the original poems, discussing any differences. They then complete the empathy task.

Comparing how characters are presented

Key ideas

- Although Chaucer wrote *The Canterbury Tales* over 600 years ago, we can relate his characters to modern ones.

ACTIVITY 2  tweakit

How does it work?

Students use descriptions of characters to draw and annotate each of them and then make comparisons in the treatment of them.

Try this!

Students can use PowerPoint to create an image of each character and annotate it with details from the text in speech or thought bubbles round them. They should add annotations to show how Chaucer uses physical details to imply character.

Or this! (to stretch and challenge students)

Use drawings or PowerPoint as the basis for a discussion and writing task on Chaucer's use of satire.

ACTIVITY 3  tweakit

How does it work?

Students use their knowledge of Chaucer's characters to imagine them as current celebrities and write a 'gossip' column about them.

Try this!

Students imagine one of the characters is appearing on a celebrity interview show. They should write the script of their conversation with the celebrity host, making sure they behave as Chaucer has depicted them.

Or this!

Students imagine one of the characters is appearing on a radio phone-in show and write a script in which three different listeners phone in to ask them questions, which they answer in a manner true to Chaucer's description.

Comparing the feelings described

Key ideas

- Poems can be linked by the emotions a writer expresses; for example, Thomas Hardy's 'The Darkling Thrush' and 'Beeny Cliff' both swing between sadness and optimism.

 **tweakit**

How does it work?

Two different grids are presented. One lists feelings for which students find appropriate quotations; the other lists quotations which students match with feelings.

Try this!

Students complete the grids using **Activity Sheet 1.4.2**.

Or this!

On a copy of the poems, students highlight all the words related to feelings and emotions. They then create word sets of the different feelings or emotions that are mentioned. Finally, for each emotion or feeling identified, they write a sentence beginning, for example, 'Loneliness is...' using an idea from the poem(s).

ACTIVITY 5  **tweakit**

How does it work?

Students design masks to convey the changing emotions in the poems and decorate them with appropriate words and phrases. They then 'interview' the poet about his use of emotional language.

Try this!

Students re-write one of the poems as a dramatic monologue in prose, retaining the emotions. Use quotations where appropriate.

Or this!

Students write a letter in character as the narrator to a close friend, describing their feelings about the poem's event. They should use quotations where appropriate.

Comparing situations

Key ideas

- Although the situation in two poems may be different, the effects created can be very different. (For example, two of Robert Browning's poems, 'Evelyn Hope' and 'Porphyria's Lover', describe a common situation but the feelings expressed are very different.)

ACTIVITY 6  **tweakit**

How does it work?

Students are asked to dramatize the situations in the poems either through a short playscript set in an afterlife or a dramatic monologue.

Try this!

Students work in pairs to produce either a newspaper headline and story about 'Porphyria's Lover' or a blog from the man in 'Evelyn Hope' in which he confesses his feelings for the dead girl and justifies himself.

Or this!

When performing their monologue (Activity 6b), students can record their performance using **Record & Playback 1.4.4** to facilitate peer and self-assessment.

ACTIVITY 7  tweakit

How does it work?

Students complete a spider diagram **(Activity Sheet 1.4.3)** looking at the situation, motives and feelings of the male narrators, and portrayal of the woman in each poem. They are then asked to make comparisons based on this.

Try this!

Students work in pairs to create a 'timeline' for each poem, showing how the situation develops. They then compare them, noting similarities and differences.

Or this!

Students work in groups as a crime investigation unit looking at unexpected deaths. They will need to examine each poem for clues about motivation and any other information they can find. They should prepare a summary report for the Crown Prosecution Service – not more than one side of A4 paper.

Comparing the use of language

Key ideas

- A writer's use of language features can give them an individual style, even when writing on different subjects.
- Christina Rossetti uses simple language with few long words to express profound ideas.

ACTIVITY 8  tweakit

How does it work?

Students use the table of language features on page 44 to help them highlight the way these are used in Christina Rossetti's 'In the Willow Shade' and 'Cousin Kate', followed by discussion of reasons for their use and the effects they have on the reader.

Try this!

Students can complete this exercise using **Activity Sheet 1.4.4** and **Activity 1.4.5** which has a copy of the poems with instructions for annotation.

Or this! (for lower ability)

Students work in pairs on a cloze version of a poem, with dictionaries. They select the missing words from a group of synonyms at the side of the page and re-write part, or all, of the poem using these. They compare their version with the original and discuss why the writer chose the words in the original version.

ACTIVITY 9

How does it work?

Students are asked to write four paragraphs about Christina Rossetti's 'In the Willow Shade' and 'Cousin Kate', comparing sound patterning, imagery, emotions and personal response.

Try this!

Students work in groups of four, with each pair responsible for a different aspect of the poems. Those responsible for sound patterning should find suitable percussion instruments to create sound effects. Those responsible for imagery should find appropriate pictures to illustrate the images. They can then either perform the poem using their 'props' or put together a PowerPoint presentation using words, colours, pictures and music or sound effects.

Writing comparisons

Key ideas

- Students will need to link two poems by the same author in their assessment. The situations described may be different but language and feelings may be common to both, or the subject matter may be related but the language and feelings different.

ACTIVITY 10

How does it work?

Students are directed to discuss two poems from their selection side by side, decide how they are linked and highlight comparisons and contrasts.

Try this!

Students work in pairs to create a Venn diagram for the pair of poems, showing where they overlap and where they are separate.

ACTIVITY 11

How does it work?

Students complete a grid to show similarities and differences between two poems they have chosen, with supporting evidence in the form of quotations. They use this as the basis for an assessment task.

Try this!

Students can use the grid on **Activity Sheet 1.4.6** to complete this activity.

Or this!

Students work in pairs or small groups to design a 'millionaire' style quiz game, where the possible answers are related to comparisons and contrasts in pairs of poems. The questions should be graded from easy to difficult. Harder questions can relate to evidence and to quotations.

Competitors have three lifelines. A CD of suitable music could provide tension. This could be done as a PowerPoint.

Ideas for plenaries

- From their work on the poems, students have five minutes to brainstorm their views of the writer's character in pairs or small groups. The teacher pulls ideas together on the board from students' feedback. This can be followed up with research homework using online biographies of the poet.
- Students use their spider diagrams and grids from their main activity and place these round the room. They then examine each other's work and discuss any different ideas. They choose one idea they like, with reasons. This could be done on 'voting slips' with a secret ballot.
- Present a quotation about the chosen poet's work. Students have five minutes to prepare a speed debate and 30 seconds for each group to put their point of view. (This can be followed up with homework, perhaps a shortened form of an assessment task.)
- Students project their grids from Activity 11 (**Activity Sheet 1.4.6**) on to the whiteboard and explain their choices to the class.

Unit 2

Modern Drama

What you need to know

Unit 2 of the OCR GCSE English Literature specification covers Modern Drama, which is assessed through a written exam. The unit counts for 25% of the total GCSE mark.

Students are expected to study one of six texts:

- *The History Boys* by Alan Bennett
- *Hobson's Choice* by Harold Brighouse
- *A View from the Bridge* by Arthur Miller
- *An Inspector Calls* by J.B. Priestley
- *Educating Rita* by Willy Russell
- *Journey's End* by R. C. Sherriff

Students answer one exam question on one of these texts. The exam will last **45 minutes**.

At the Higher Tier, the exam question will be worth a maximum of 40 marks.

At the Foundation Tier, it will be worth a maximum of 27 marks.

Question types

There will be a choice of two types of question in Unit 2.

- **Passage-based questions**
  These questions are presented along with an extract from the play printed in the exam booklet. Students are expected to focus on this passage, although they will also need to show knowledge of the play as a whole. In a passage-based question, students are often asked to identify what is particularly dramatic about the extract they have been given and so this concept should be clearly covered with them beforehand. Students may also be asked to focus on their reaction to the text as a member of the audience.

- **Questions requiring comment, criticism and analysis**

  These essay questions will ask students to look at the play as a whole, reading with insight, discussing how ideas are reinforced through language, structure and form, and supporting their points with relevant quotations. In this type of question, students may be asked to consider the importance or significance of a particular character in the play, and should consider what the character reveals or represents rather than producing a character study.

Students writing at Foundation level will be presented with bullet point prompts and will be able to write their answer directly onto the exam paper. Higher Tier questions will not include prompts and candidates will answer their question in an exam booklet.

Film versions

You may wish to show students a film version of the play they are studying, and there are good versions of many of the prescribed plays. However, it is important to ensure students are made aware of the fact that film versions can differ from the original script, and that they should not write about the film version in their exam.

Assessment Objectives

The Assessment Objectives covered in this unit are:

AO1

Respond to texts critically and imaginatively; select and evaluate relevant textual detail to illustrate and support interpretations.

AO2

Explain how language, structure and form contribute to writers' presentation of ideas, themes and settings.

Assessment Objectives

AO1

- Respond to texts critically and imaginatively.
- Select and evaluate relevant textual detail to illustrate and support interpretations.

AO2

- Explain how language, structure and form contribute to writers' presentation of ideas, themes and settings.

Ideas for starters

- Introduce key words from this chapter by playing dictionary races with students in which they have to find the meaning of unfamiliar words first.
- Identify a key character from the play studied. Ask students to work in pairs to create three questions they would ask the character if they had the opportunity. Then assume that role yourself and respond to the questions posed.
- At any given point in the study of a play, list ten important things that have happened so far but put them in the wrong order. Students work in pairs to sequence events correctly.

Approaching a passage-based question

Key ideas

- Passage-based questions refer specifically to the play extract printed in the exam booklet. Although students will need to have knowledge of the whole play, their answer should be focused on this passage.
- Students should read the question first, then read the passage closely and then read the question again (annotating as necessary).
- **Presentation 2.1.1** can be used to cover this section with students.

Understanding key terms

Key ideas

- Students will be expected to use key terms comfortably in their answers. These include: insight, interpretations, themes, setting, protagonist, tone and context.

ACTIVITY 1  tweakit

How does it work?
Students match the key term in the left hand column of the grid with the correct definition in the right hand column.

Try this!
Students work in pairs matching the terms to the right definition which then leads into whole class discussion and correction.
Interactive 2.1.1 can be used to aid them in completing the task.

Or this! (for higher ability)
Give students only one column of the grid and ask them to either create their own definitions for the key terms or to identify the key terms using the definitions.

ACTIVITY 2  tweakit

How does it work?
Students read the five student responses on *Educating Rita* on page 55 carefully and then match them to at least one of the key terms identified in Activity 1.

Try this!
Students work individually matching the key terms to the student responses and then share their answers with a partner. Answers can then be corrected and discussed as a whole class.

Or this!
Once answers have been corrected, ask students to find a supporting quotation from the opening pages of the play to reinforce the point made in each of the student responses.

Or this!
Students identify one of the student responses and work on developing and extending the response by adding an additional paragraph using the PEE formula.

Reading with insight

Key ideas
• Students need to show they have read their chosen play with insight, i.e. that they have looked below the surface meaning and understood the subtext.

ACTIVITY 3  tweakit

How does it work?
Students read the extract from *Educating Rita* on page 56 carefully and then identify which of the words in the box best describe Frank.

Try this!

Students work in pairs to identify which of the words best describe Frank, justifying their answers. Ask pairs to feed back so you can correct answers and discuss them as a whole class.

Or this! (for lower ability)

Students use dictionaries to first find out the meaning of any words they do not know. They then work in pairs to identify which of the words best describe Frank, justifying their answers.

Supporting your ideas with quotations

Key ideas

- When answering passage-based questions, students are expected to select words and phrases from the passage to support their ideas accurately.
- Examiners look for the ability to analyse how a writer uses language to create effects. Students should understand why certain words and phrases are used.

ACTIVITY 4  tweakit

How does it work?

Students match a word from the seven listed to the correct quotation from *Educating Rita*.

Try this!

Students work in pairs matching each of the seven words that describe Frank to the correct supporting quotation in a card sort activity. Correct and discuss answers as a whole class.

Or this!

The task could also be completed using the matching activity in **Interactive 2.1.2**.

Or this!

Students work in pairs reading the quotations aloud in the way they think Frank might speak them. Volunteers speak these aloud to the whole class who vote for the best delivery. Watch the performance by Michael Caine as Frank and compare.

ACTIVITY 5  tweakit

How does it work?

Students use two or three of the quotations provided in Activity 4 to write a paragraph explaining how the playwright portrays Frank to make the opening of the play interesting for the audience.

Try this!

Model for students how to develop the student response provided, embedding one of the quotations provided and exploring the portrayal of Frank. Then ask students to work individually doing the same but using a different quotation.

Or this! (for mixed ability groups)
Divide the class into smaller groups and assign each a quotation
from the list provided. Students work together to write a paragraph
developing the student response given, embedding their supporting
quotation and exploring how the portrayal of Frank at this stage
makes the opening interesting. Share outcomes as a whole class and
evaluate which responses are the most successful and why.

ACTIVITY 6

How does it work?
Students complete a cloze exercise in which they use the words
provided to fill in the blanks in a student response on *The History
Boys*.

Try this! (for higher ability)
Ask students to work in pairs to complete the cloze exercise but
without the answers. Discuss and correct answers as a whole class.
Compare outcomes with the answers provided on page 58.

Or this! (for lower ability)
Use dictionary races to clarify the meaning of the words provided
as the answers. If necessary, revisit the parts of speech. Then ask
students to work in pairs to select the right word for each gap in the
student response. Discuss and correct as a whole class.

Or this!
The activity can also be completed using **Interactive 2.1.3**.

ACTIVITY 7

How does it work?
In 7a, students work in pairs discussing what they learn about Rita
from the language she uses in the extract from *Educating Rita*, using
the bullet points and key words to focus their thoughts. In 7b, students
write a paragraph in which they explain their interpretation of Rita,
based on the language she uses in the extract. They should make use
of the words provided and supporting quotations.

Try this!
Students read the passage closely and then work in pairs to identify
key words and phrases that interest them. They then make notes
about each of these in relation to the bullet points, using the key
words as a support. Take feedback and discuss as a whole group.

Or this! (for lower ability)
Students research a Liverpudlian accent on the Internet and then
read the extract attempting the accent themselves. Share these as a
whole class and vote for the best performance. Compare them with the
performance of Julie Walters in the film version of *Educating Rita*.

Or this! (for higher ability)

Students evaluate which term – 'freak' or 'half caste' – is the most effective in terms of encapsulating Rita's situation.

Or this! (for mixed ability groups)

Provide a weak sample response to Activity 7b, which explains what is revealed about Rita by the language she uses, at grade D level. Ask students to work in pairs to improve it. Take feedback and discuss as a shared writing exercise.

Or this! (for lower ability)

Model the PEE formula for Activity 7b and then ask students to complete the task on their own. They should share their responses with a partner who assesses it.

Try This!

Teaching notes

- Activities 1 and 3 focus on students' understanding of character and are good for revision purposes. Encourage students to be as creative and humorous as they can! Activity 2 is more flexible and can be done as students read chronologically through the text, pausing to create their 'tweets' as they go, tracking changes in the characters. Alternatively, it can be done once the text has been read in full to revisit these changes in the characters as a revision tool.

- Activities 4 and 5 draw on specific television programmes and genre types as a teaching aid. There is an obvious link with Media Studies here. Don't forget about how useful related documentaries can be too, in terms of clarifying for students where and when the plays were set. Use of such an approach works better when what students are looking for is made explicit at the outset and an appropriate grid/proforma is used to help structure students' thoughts and note-taking.

- Activity 5 allows students to work in groups and to reinforce their understanding of the action, theme and portrayal of character in a way that is imaginative and engaging.

Ideas for plenaries

- Create a rolling PowerPoint of images related closely and not so obviously to the section of the play studied during the lesson. Flash each image up for ten seconds and ask students to explain the connection with the play's themes, characters, setting, etc.

- Distribute sticky notes to students. Ask them to rate the extent to which they feel they have met the learning objectives in the chapter on a scale of 1 – 10 by writing this on the sticky note with a question about any area of the lesson they feel unsure about. Discuss these concerns in subsequent lessons. (This could form a useful starter.)

Assessment Objectives

AO1

- Respond to texts critically and imaginatively.
- Select and evaluate relevant textual detail to illustrate and support interpretations.

AO2

- Explain how language, structure and form contribute to writers' presentation of ideas, themes and settings.

Ideas for starters

- Ask students to discuss in pairs the three most important points from the previous lesson for one minute. Take feedback and discuss as a whole class, evaluating what the most significant point is.
- Get students to attempt the accents of characters from the play they are studying and celebrate these by sharing them – good and not so good! – with the class.

Understanding the significance of characters

Key ideas

- When answering a general question on a play, students will also be expected to read with insight, support their points with relevant quotations and discuss how ideas are reinforced through language, structure and form.
- For general questions, students will need to show a clear understanding of the whole play, especially characters and how they represent various viewpoints. **Presentation 2.2.1** can be used to explore this question type more fully.
- Some characters have a function beyond interacting with other characters; for example, as a narrator.
- A dramatic tragedy (e.g. *A View from the Bridge*) often involves the death of the main character and a sense of foreboding running throughout the play.

ACTIVITY 1  **tweakit**

How does it work?

Students read the extract from *A View from the Bridge* and then match quotations to the themes listed.

Try this! (for higher ability)

Read the passage aloud and ask students to work in pairs to identify what they think the themes are without using the answers on page 63. Take feedback and compare outcomes as a class.

Or this! (for lower ability)

Ask students to work in pairs to define what the term 'theme' means. Take feedback and clarify. Then ask pairs to match the themes identified on page 63 with relevant quotations from the extract. Correct and discuss as a group.

ACTIVITY 2    tweakit

How does it work?

In the core task, students write a paragraph about how the extract identified clearly establishes that the play is a tragedy. In the extension task, students research the idea of the 'chorus' in drama, responding to specific prompts.

Try this! (for higher ability)

Students discuss the core task in pairs first. They then write their paragraph, which they later share with a partner for peer assessment.

Or this! (for mixed ability groups)

Discuss as a class which quotations are most relevant to the core task. Provide a response for students at grade C level, with key words deleted. Ask them to fill in the blanks.

Or this! (for higher ability)

Students work in groups using computer and Internet access to track the history and development of the 'chorus' as a dramatic device, creating a timeline with the information they find which they formally present to the group. Vote for the best interpretation and display this in the form of a washing line in the classroom.

Or this! (for mixed ability groups)

Students work in pairs using the Internet to research the idea of the chorus. You could also use the information sheet (**Activity Sheet 2.2.1**) to support students where necessary. Take feedback and discuss as a whole class.

Portraying character through language

Key ideas

- In their answers, students need to analyse the use of vocabulary, phrasing, tone, style and dramatic impact.
- 'Analyse' means explaining how and why things are said and what this reveals about characters.

ACTIVITY 3    tweakit

How does it work?

Students plan a response based on a character from the text they are studying, explaining his or her dramatic impact in the play.

Try this! (with a mixed ability group)

Ask students to work in pairs to define what 'dramatic impact' means. Take feedback and clarify. Model how to plan such a response for one of the characters in the play studied using **Activity Sheet 2.2.2**, and then ask students to work in pairs to plan a similar response from a list of selected characters.

Or this!

Focus on collaboratively planning a response based on one character. Then divide the class into smaller groups and get them to act out a freeze frame from a specific moment in the play for each of the points in their plan. Share these as a class. 'Free' the chosen character to walk around at certain points in the freeze frame to discuss his or her feelings towards the others in the frame at that time and the impact of the scene on the audience.

Or this! (for higher ability)

Ask students to work in pairs to identify a character from their chosen play. Once the have completed their plan ask them to evaluate the three most significant points they have identified with a justification for each.

ACTIVITY 4  tweakit

How does it work?

Students complete a cloze exercise in which they use words provided to fill in the blanks in a student response which successfully analyses use of language in *The History Boys*.

Try this!

Students can complete the activity on the whiteboard using **Interactive 2.2.1**.

Or this! (for higher ability)

Ask students to work in pairs to fill in the blanks without the answers given. Take feedback and discuss outcomes as a class. Alternatively, ask students to complete the exercise as presented, but then consider alternatives to the answers provided.

Or this! (for lower ability)

Once students have completed the cloze exercise, ask them to draw a visual representation of the metaphor to reinforce their learning. They should then share outcomes with a partner and as a class.

ACTIVITY 5  tweakit

How does it work?

Students write a paragraph explaining how their selected character adds dramatic impact to the play they are studying. This should be based on one of the points made in the plan they created in Activity 3.

Try this!

Model for students how to successfully complete the task. Then ask them to work in pairs to do the same for an alternative point on their plan. Get students to share their outcomes with another pair through peer assessment.

Or this! (for higher ability)

Provide students with three sample responses and ask them to work in pairs to rank them in order, justifying why they feel one is better than the other. Take feedback and discuss as a class.

Character development

Key ideas

- In answering a question on character, students should remember to consider their role throughout the play and how their character develops.
- They should also consider how the audience's opinion of the character may change.
- Quotations should be used as springboards to develop deeper insight into the text.

ACTIVITY 6  **tweakit**

How does it work?

Students complete a table which analyses the portrayal of Mr Birling from *An Inspector Calls* based on a specific extract.

Try this!

Ask students to work in pairs to complete the table (**Activity Sheet 2.2.3**). Take feedback, discuss and correct as a whole group.

Or this! (for higher ability)

Give students the first row example and then the main points of the first column only so that they complete the 'quotation' and 'comment/analysis' columns in pairs. Take feedback, discuss and correct as a whole group.

Or this! (for a mixed ability group)

Students identify a key character at a specific moment in the play. They work in pairs to make a list of questions they would like to ask them. An able volunteer then assumes this character in the hot seat and students ask him or her their questions.

ACTIVITY 7  **tweakit**

How does it work?

Students write a paragraph analysing the unsympathetic portrayal of Mr Birling in *An Inspector Calls* based on the extract given, using the completed grid from Activity 6 as a reference.

Try this!

Students work in pairs to write their analysis which they then share with another pair who assesses their efforts.

Or this! (for a mixed ability group)

Students select images taken from newspapers and magazines that they feel suitably relate to the points raised about Mr Birling in the table from Activity 6. They should create a collage of these, adding supporting quotations and analysis.

ACTIVITY 8

 **tweakit**

How does it work?

Students identify two or three key speeches made by a central protagonist from the play they have studied at different points in the play. They then explore how that character is portrayed in these key extracts.

Try this!

Work with students in identifying an appropriate speech by one of the main protagonists from the play they have studied. Then model how to analyse its significance in terms of what it reveals about that character and how the playwright manipulates the reaction of the audience (use **Activity Sheet 2.2.4**). Students can go on to select an additional speech and do the same.

Or this! (for higher ability)

Assign different key speeches to different groups of students. Ask them to create their own table, like the example in Activity 6, which they subsequently give to another group to complete.

Ideas for plenaries

- Display a quotation about a director's portrayal of a character, their interpretation of the play or the performance of an actor that chimes with an area of the text currently being studied. Ask students to work in pairs to discuss this quotation and their reaction to it. Share outcomes as a whole class.
- In a lesson focused on the portrayal of character, divide the class into two groups. Ask one group to list reasons why they feel sympathy for the character and the other to list reasons why they do not. Share these outcomes in a short, improvised debate.

Unit 3

Prose from Different Cultures

What you need to know

Prose from Different Cultures is covered by Unit 3 of the OCR GCSE English Literature specification, and is assessed through a written exam. Like the other three units, it counts for 25% of the total GCSE mark.

Students are expected to study one of six different cultures prose texts:

- *Of Mice and Men* by John Steinbeck
- *To Kill a Mockingbird* by Harper Lee
- *Anita and Me* by Meera Syal
- *Paddy Clarke Ha Ha Ha* by Roddy Doyle
- *Tsotsi* by Athol Fugard
- *The Joy Luck Club* by Amy Tan

Students will be presented with two questions on each set text, and must choose one of these to answer. The exam will last 45 minutes. Students should be advised to spend some of this time carefully choosing which of the two questions on their set text they will answer.

At the Higher Tier, the exam question will be worth a maximum of 40 marks.

At the Foundation Tier, it will be worth a maximum of 27 marks.

Question types

Unit 3 gives a choice of two types of question.

- **Passage-based questions**

  For passage-based questions, students are provided with an extract from the prose text printed on the exam paper and are expected to focus on this extract in their answer. However, they should also show knowledge of the novel as a whole and an understanding of why the passage is significant.

- **Questions requiring comment, criticism and analysis**
  In this question, students should refer to the novel as a whole, rather than focusing on a particular extract. The question may relate to a specific episode in the novel, or it may involve a particular theme or character, so students should be prepared for all of these possibilities. They will need to read with insight and support their points with relevant quotations.

Students writing at Foundation level will be presented with bullet point prompts and will be able to write their answer directly on to the exam paper. Higher Tier questions will not include prompts and candidates will answer their question in a separate exam booklet.

Context

As part of their study of different cultures prose texts, students will be expected to have some understanding of the contextual issues surrounding their chosen novel. They will not need to undertake extensive research, but should be equipped with an understanding of key issues and how these issues are relevant to the text. However, students should be clear that they will not receive marks for recounting historical and cultural facts without reference to the novel, and should always focus their answer on the question itself.

Assessment Objectives

The Assessment Objectives covered in this unit are:

AO2

Explain how language, structure and form contribute to writers' presentation of ideas, themes and settings

AO4

Relate texts to their social, cultural and historical contexts; explain how texts have been influential and significant to self and other readers in different contexts and at different times.

Assessment Objectives

AO2

- Explain how language, structure and form contribute to writers' presentation of ideas, themes and settings.

AO4

- Relate texts to their social, cultural and historical contexts.

- Explain how texts have been influential and significant to self and other readers in different contexts and at different times.

Ideas for starters

- Revisit key points about the text by playing *Bingo*! List twelve key words related to the text studied. Students then select ten of these randomly and write them down. Select a word and ask a related question to review previous learning. The first student with all ten words called out by the teacher calls 'Bingo!' to win.
- Revisit your CD collection! Identify snippets of songs that relate to key issues from the text studied. Play these to students who listen carefully and explain the connection. Students do the same thing for homework, bringing a song of their own which they feel has a connection with the text. Three or four students play their songs to the class as the starter for the next series of lessons.

Choosing a passage-based question

Key ideas

- When choosing a passage-based question, students will need to read the extract closely to explore character, theme or effect. They will also need to consider language and form.
- Students need to show an appreciation of context – when the text was written and where it is set.
- Students should be prepared to annotate their exam question – one approach is provided on pages 78–79. You could use **Presentation 3.1.1** to introduce this approach to students.

ACTIVITY 1    **tweakit**

How does it work?
Students annotate the questions provided to reveal the extent to which they understand and appreciate exactly what is being asked of them.

Try this!

Students work in pairs to annotate the questions (**Activity Sheet 3.1.1**) and feed back their responses leading into whole class discussion and correction.

Or this! (for higher ability)

Having done the above, students work in pairs to create their own questions in the style of those annotated for a particular passage of their choice. They then pass these to another pair for them to consider and annotate.

Showing awareness of differences

Key ideas

• For different cultures texts, students need to show that they understand how characters' attitudes differ from their own.

ACTIVITY 2  tweakit

How does it work?

Students read the four extracts carefully and identify the prejudice evident in each.

Try this!

Students work in pairs to identify the prejudice. Take feedback and discuss as a whole class.

Or this!

Ask students to identify alternative quotations for the prejudices identified in the four extracts and to identify any other forms of prejudice that exist in the novel (with related quotations).

Language choices and quotations

Key ideas

• Students need to support their points with quotations and discuss them. They need to show awareness of how the writer uses language.

ACTIVITY 3  tweakit

How does it work?

Students complete a grid which identifies a quotation and language feature and then analyses its effect on the reader.

Try this!

Ask students to read the extract carefully and then work in pairs to complete the table (**Activity Sheet 3.1.2**). Discuss and correct answers as a whole class.

Or this! (for lower ability)

Revisit figurative language in a card sort activity. Once corrected, ask students to complete the table. Take feedback, discuss and correct.

Then ask students to select related images from newspapers and magazines. They should make a collage to represent the points made in the table with quotations and explanatory notes around the images.

Or this! (for higher ability)

Give students the table with only the first column completed. They should then work in pairs to complete it. Take feedback, correct and discuss.

ACTIVITY 4  **tweakit**

How does it work?

Students use the grid completed in Activity 3 and the quotations from *Of Mice and Men* provided on page 81 to write a paragraph explaining how the writer successfully describes Maycomb as a town in decline.

Try this!

Model for students how to use one of the quotations and the first row of the grid to write a paragraph. Then ask them to work in pairs to write their own which they share with another pair for assessment.

Or this! (for higher ability)

Provide a Grade B response and ask students to assess it using the exam mark scheme criteria. Then ask them to work individually to develop it into a Grade A or A* response.

Different social and cultural settings

Key ideas

- When looking at different cultures texts, students should consider how society's attitude varies according to time and place.
- Students should focus primarily on the printed extract in exams, but also expand their answer to show wider knowledge and understanding of the text as a whole.

ACTIVITY 5  **tweakit**

How does it work?

Students read the quotations from *Of Mice and Men* and then decide which create sympathy for Curley's wife and which create dislike for her.

Try this!

Create cards with each quotation written on them. Students work in pairs to arrange these according to whether they create sympathy or dislike for Curley's wife. Alternatively, they could do this using **Interactive 3.1.1**. Take feedback, correct and discuss.

Or this! (for higher ability)

Once students have identified which quotations accurately create sympathy or dislike for Curley's wife, they should debate and evaluate which of the comments are the most powerful in terms of creating sympathy or dislike.

ACTIVITY 6  tweakit

How does it work?

Students select the correct words provided to fill in the gaps in the student response on page 83.

Try this!

Students read the student response and then work in pairs to select the right word to fill the gaps. (They could do this using **Interactive 3.1.2**.) Take feedback, correct and discuss answers as a class.

Or this! (for higher ability)

Ask students to complete the task without access to the answers. Take feedback and discuss.

Or this! (for higher ability)

Ask students to work in pairs to create their own cloze activity, like the one for Curley's wife, but this time for another character and another prejudice. They should pass this to another pair for completion.

Different political and historical settings

Key ideas

*   Novels set in the past often reflect the different social and political viewpoints of that time. (For example, *Tsotsi* is set in a South African township during apartheid.)

ACTIVITY 7  tweakit

How does it work?

In Activity 7a, students read the passage and then match quotations from it to the bullet points about life for black people under the apartheid regime. In Activity 7b, students explore and analyse a particular phrase used by Athol Fugard to describe Tsotsi. In an extension task, students write a paragraph in response to specific prompts in which they explain how Tsotsi is a metaphor for South Africa at that time.

Try this!

Ask students to read the extract carefully and then work in pairs to match quotations to the points which Fugard is making about life for black people living under apartheid (**Activity Sheet 3.1.3**). Take feedback, correct and discuss.

Or this! (for lower ability)

Give students the quotations and ask them to match these to the points made. Take feedback, correct and discuss.

Or this!

For Activity 7b, students work in pairs to explore and analyse the quotation. Pairs then snowball into fours to share and compare responses.

Or this!

Once clarified, students represent what they understand by the quotation in a visual image framed within a mirror. Share and have students nominate their favourite image.

Or this! (for a mixed ability group)

To complete the extension activity, provide students with a sample response with key words missing and ask them to work in pairs to fill in the blanks.

Or this!

Students work in pairs to identify words to describe *Tsotsi* based on the letters that spell 'South Africa'. They should then work individually to write their response inside a map of South Africa on a sheet of A4.

ACTIVITY 8    **tweakit**

How does it work?

Students analyse the use of simile in Fugard's description of Tsotsi.

Try this!

Students work in pairs to analyse the effect of the two similes used which they then share with another pair for peer assessment.

Or this! (for lower ability)

Revisit what a simile is. Model how to analyse the effect of the first simile and then ask students to analyse the second one which they can share with a partner for peer assessment.

Ideas for plenaries

- Ask students to work in pairs to rewrite the last paragraph of the text they are studying on mini-whiteboards in five minutes. Share outcomes and discuss choices made.

- Ask students to work in pairs to summarize the text in a ten word sentence exactly or analyse a character in an eight word sentence exactly. Share outcomes.

- Ask an able volunteer to take the hot seat as the author of the text studied. Students then ask questions about specific sections they have read and analysed in terms of what the author's intention was.

Assessment Objectives

AO2

- Explain how language, structure and form contribute to writers' presentation of ideas, themes and settings.

AO4

- Relate texts to their social, cultural and historical contexts.

- Explain how texts have been influential and significant to self and other readers in different contexts and at different times.

Ideas for starters

- Ask students to describe their own cultural identity: where they were born, what they believe and how they are perceived by others. You may wish to model how this can be done sensitively.
- Write the word 'culture' on the board and ask students to devise an acrostic poem which defines the term or their own cultural identity.
- Display a series of pictures showing scenes from different cultures (America, India, Africa, Ireland, etc.) and encourage students to gather as much information as they can about that culture from each picture. The name of the country in which the novel they are studying can then be written on the board and the students can create a spider diagram about their knowledge of this country and culture.
- 'Who am I?': Students write a monologue in the 'voice' of one of the characters in the novel they are studying. The character defines himself or herself and describes what is important to him or her, without saying specifically who he or she is. The rest of the class has to guess who the character is and discuss what they have learned about that character.
- Challenge students in pairs to prepare a flow diagram similar to the one on page 88 for a character in the novel they are studying. Lower ability students studying *Tsotsi*, *Of Mice and Men* or *Anita and Me* can complete **Interactives 3.2.2**, **3.2.3** and **3.2.4**, which look at the characters of Tsotsi, George and Meena.

Commenting on texts

Key ideas

- In the exam, students may choose to answer questions requiring comment, critical evaluation or analysis of the novel they are studying. (You may find **Presentation 3.2.1** useful in introducing comment, criticism and analysis questions.)

Understanding context

Key ideas

- In studying different cultures texts, students should explore context: setting, characters' beliefs and the expectations of their communities.

ACTIVITY 1

 **tweakit**

How does it work?

Students read a list of contextual factors and then write down or tick any that apply to the specific novel they are studying.

Try this!

Students should discuss specifically what they know about the contextual features of their novel. Then assign groups to research an aspect of the context and prepare a PowerPoint presentation clearly connecting their research to the novel. For example, a class studying *Of Mice and Men* might have one group looking at the politics of 1930s America; another at gender roles; another at the lives of migrant workers; another at the popular novels and literary movements of that time; another at the life and work of John Steinbeck and the last at the geography of the Salinas, California area.

Or this!

Students should write a paragraph summing up what they have learned about the context and how this influences their understanding of the novel.

Or this! (for lower ability)

Students should make a chart of three or four major contextual issues, such as location, time period, politics and social issues and write down one piece of evidence from the novel about each.

Narrative voice

Key ideas

- There are different types of narrative voice. The two main types are first-person and third-person narrators.
- First-person narrators are characters in the novel, they use I/we, may be informal and have gaps in their knowledge of events. Novels may have multiple first-person narrators.
- Third-person narrators use he/she/they, may be omniscient, and are usually more formally and objectively written.
- Novels may also have unreliable narrators, whose perceptions cannot be trusted.

ACTIVITY 2

 tweakit

How does it work?

Students read about narrative voice. (**Presentation 3.2.2** can be used to introduce this topic.) After reading a series of short excerpts from the set novels, they work in pairs to sort them into first- or third-person narrators (**Interactive 3.2.1**). They discuss with their partner what their impressions are of these narrators.

Try this!

Ask the students to experiment with the excerpts: for example, by changing them from first to third person. How does that change the novel? Students should then draw up a chart explaining the advantages and disadvantages of first-person and third-person narration.

Or this!

Students should analyse a longer excerpt from the novel they are studying in which they identify key features of the narrator. Ask them to look at the narrator's vocabulary, point of view (from one character's point of view or many?), gaps in knowledge (if any) or omniscient, relationship to reader (is the reader directly addressed like a friend?).

ACTIVITY 3

 tweakit

How does it work?

Students learn the definition of an 'unreliable narrator'. They then read a short extract from *Anita and Me* and consider if that narrator is unreliable or not. As an extension task for more able students, they are encouraged to write their own piece using an unreliable narrator.

Try this!

Students complete the activity and then discuss as a class why a writer might use an unreliable narrator and what effect this can have on a reader.

Or this! (for higher ability)

Encourage students to write their own short story from an unusual narrative point of view (for example, a very young child; an uninvolved bystander; even an animal!). How does this affect their story?

Or this!

Several of the narrators in the novels are children. Ask students to identify one or more passages in the novel they are studying which would be very different if written from an adult point of view.

Or this!

Students complete a paragraph in which they write about the author's choice of narrative voice. It should include evidence from the novel and an explanation of how it influences the reader's understanding and enjoyment of the novel.

Characterization

Key ideas

- When analysing characters, students should consider how they are described, their dialogue, importance to the plot and how they interact with other characters.
- Main protagonists usually go on an emotional or psychological journey in a novel; for example, Paddy Clarke's development in *Paddy Clarke Ha Ha Ha*.

Setting and culture

Key ideas

- Setting is important to our understanding of characters and their behaviour.

ACTIVITY 4  tweakit

How does it work?

Students read an extract from *Anita and Me* and analyse Meena's parents' attitude to their home in New Delhi. They are then asked to find a contrasting passage in the novel which shows how the characters feel about Tollington, and to produce a paragraph closely comparing the two extracts.

Try this!

Students may choose to compare the opening pages of the novel with the description of the New Delhi home. Ask them to closely annotate the opening pages for any positive or negative imagery and techniques that the author uses (metaphor, alliteration, simile, oppositions).

Or this! (for lower ability)

Key words and phrases from the contrasting passages, either projected or written on slips of paper, are presented to the students. Ask them to place the phrases either under the heading 'Tollington' or 'New Delhi' in their exercise books and then write a paragraph comparing the two. Remind them of key 'compare and contrast' words ('however,' 'on the other hand,' etc.).

ACTIVITY 5  tweakit

How does it work?

Students choose a passage from the novel they are studying in which location is important. They closely analyse the techniques the author uses and then discuss with a partner how the location affects the characters in the novel.

Try this!

There are many passages from each of the set novels which could be used for this exercise. A few examples are: *The Joy Luck Club* (the Huangs' house or the description of Waverly Place; *Tsotsi* (Tsotsi's gang walking through the township at twilight; *To Kill a Mockingbird* (the descriptions of Maycomb and the Radley place; *Of Mice and Men* (the bunkhouse at the beginning of Chapter 2 or the Crooks' room at the beginning of Chapter 4) or *Paddy Clarke Ha Ha Ha* (the Donnelly barn). Emphasize that they are looking at how the location affects the characters.

Or this!

Encourage the students to write two short, vivid passages, using a variety of techniques, about a place they like and one they dislike. Have them exchange passages with their partner and highlight the techniques used in each other's writing.

Exploring themes

Key ideas

- A theme is a significant idea that an author explores in his or her work.
- Novels can contain multiple themes.
- Common themes in 20th and 21st century novels are loneliness, isolation and personal identity.
- Childhood is another common theme and can include: community, growing up and changing, family, friendships, education and beliefs.

ACTIVITY 6  **tweakit**

How does it work?

Students read a definition of a theme and then consider a list of possible themes. They select which themes they believe apply to the novel they are studying.

Try this! (for mixed ability groups)

Focus on several of the possible themes from the novel. Assign students to mixed ability groups, with one of the more able students as 'leader'. Ask each group to prepare a presentation on one of the possible themes. Their presentation should include: an A3 poster of ideas about the themes, a list of quotations, and a short PowerPoint presentation about how the theme is developed in the novel. Less able students may work on the poster, while more able students may organize the textual evidence and presentation.

Or this! (for lower ability)

Ask each student to create a visual image that represents a theme (a book for 'education'; scales of justice for 'injustice', etc.) and annotate their copy of the text with their image whenever they think that particular theme is being explored.

How does it work?

Students read about the theme of childhood and discuss the colour-coded spider diagram in the Student Book (page 90; an editable version is available on **Activity Sheet 3.2.1**). They use this as a basis for creating their own spider diagram on this or another theme. (A blank version of the spider diagram is available on **Activity Sheet 3.2.2**.)

Try this!

Model for the class ways of developing the spider diagram, encouraging them to find quotations from the novel for each of the 'arms' of the diagram. Demonstrate ways of exploring the aspects of their theme in detail.

Or this! (for lower ability)

Supply the students with quotations about childhood and have them place them around the parts of the spider diagram that they think they would support.

Or this! (for higher ability)

Students create their own detailed, colour coded spider diagram on the theme of their choice. Ask them to number the areas of their spider diagram as the first stage of planning an essay on that theme. They could then compose an essay question that they believe the information from their spider diagram could help them to answer.

Prejudice, injustice and racism

Key ideas

- The 20th century was one of great political and social change, and novels written during this time reflect this. Injustice and prejudice are common themes.
- When looking at these themes, students need to consider social attitudes at the time a book is set.

How does it work?

Students read about the themes of prejudice, injustice and racism and then answer a series of bullet point questions relating the theme of prejudice to their chosen novel.

Try this! (for less confident students)

Make sure that students are confident with the concept of 'prejudice' before beginning this task. Ask them to find evidence from newspapers of 'prejudice', 'racism' or 'injustice' which are still present in the world today.

Or this! (for higher ability)

Have students debate the following topics: 'No matter what we do, there will always be injustice in the world' or 'It is a writer's responsibility to expose racism and prejudice and encourage the reader to action'. They should include what they know about injustice and prejudice in the world and as presented in the novel they are studying.

Or this!

After answering the bullet point questions, ask the students to create a detailed essay plan to answer the following question: 'How does the author use language and characterization to explore his or her thoughts and feelings about the theme of prejudice in the novel you are studying?' Ask them to exchange plans with a partner and make at least one suggestion for improvement.

Language, structure and form

Key ideas

- Students need to show understanding of language, structure and form.
- Techniques writers use include ordering of ideas, repetition of images or connections between events and ideas, metaphor, simile, alliteration, symbolism and personification.

ACTIVITY 9  **tweakit**

How does it work?

Students read about language, structure and form, looking at the annotated questions on a passage from *To Kill a Mockingbird* on page 92. They then choose a passage from the novel they are studying (or another from *To Kill a Mockingbird*) and highlight the author's use of language. As an extension task, the students write a paragraph in the style and genre of their chosen author.

Try this!

There are a number of passages that could be chosen from the novels. Students might experiment with some of the following techniques: stream of consciousness (*Paddy Clarke Ha Ha Ha*), multiple first person narrators (*The Joy Luck Club*), colloquial first person narration (*Anita and Me*) or an apparently dispassionate third person chronological narration (*Of Mice and Men*).

Or this! (for lower ability)

Model writing the opening lines of the extension task on the board and give the students the option of using those as their first lines, which they must then complete in the same style.

Bringing together your ideas

Key ideas

- In answering the exam question, students should remember to comment, criticize and analyse, and show understanding of language, form, structure and context. They need to use evidence from the text and comment on how the author achieves his or her effects.

ACTIVITY 10

 tweakit

How does it work?

Students return to the ideas of 'comment, criticize and analyse' and complete a grid exploring how the thoughts and feelings of one of the characters in their novel are expressed at the end of the novel (**Activity Sheet 3.2.3**).

Try this!

Have the students work in pairs to complete the chart. You may wish to remind them of the flow chart on page 88 of the Student Book which could help them to identify the character's turning point and development. Encourage them to use evidence from key chapters throughout the novel.

Or this! (for mixed ability groups)

Put the students into ability groups, each group being assigned a different character to explore (though obviously the characters who are not present at the end of the novel, like Curley's wife, will not be appropriate). Assign the more complex characters to the more able groups, while the characters you have more thoroughly discussed in lessons or whose reactions are more straightforward could be covered by the less able groups.

ACTIVITY 11

 tweakit

How does it work?

Students read an extract from a student's response about Miriam in *Tsotsi*. They discuss how the extract could be extended or improved.

Try this!

Working in pairs, ask the students to return to the Assessment Objectives for this unit as described on pages 76–77 of the Student Book. When assessing the student's response, they should note when either AO2 or AO4 is being met. When suggesting additional paragraphs or improvements, they should focus on how they will be meeting one of the Assessment Objectives.

Or this!

Students write a detailed plan for their own response to the question of how the thoughts and feelings of one of the key characters in the novel they are studying are expressed at the end of the novel. On their plan they should write when they are specifically going to meet either AO2 or AO4. This essay should be completed as either a timed writing or homework assignment.

Try this!

Teaching Notes

• Focusing on Curley's wife and her life before marrying Curley, students create two role-plays. Encourage their creativity by establishing what it is like at the 'Riverside Dance Palace' and at Curley's wife's home: the time of day, who else is present, what they are wearing. What is the man's objective for saying he can get her into the movies and her mother's for discouraging her? Try having half the class working on one scene and half on the other and then contrasting them. The scenes can be recorded using **Record & Playback 3.2.1** and **Record & Playback 3.2.2** to facilitate peer and self-assessment.

• Hot-seating is a fun and effective way of encouraging empathy and insight into characters. Make sure that the students research the character they are going to 'be' and that nothing they say contradicts the facts of the novel.

• To start off their work on Activity 3, students will find information on 1930s films on **Activity Sheet 3.2.4**.

• Encourage the students to research newspaper articles from different times and places in order to capture the correct tone and form for their writing. For example, students writing an article based on *Of Mice and Men* could visit the 'Learn California' website and read actual articles from the 1930s: http://bigkylet.tripod.com/1930socialissues/id2.html. However, do warn them that some websites only provide articles at a price. Librarians can also give them guidance on archive research.

Ideas for plenaries

• Working first in pairs and then feeding back as a whole class, ask students to make a list of common problems with student responses to examination questions. Some possibilities might be: tendency to simply retell the plot; lack of literary terminology; lack of evidence from the text; little or no awareness of context. Then ask the class to honestly assess their own writing and suggest one specific target for improvement.

• 'Just a Minute': Students have one minute to speak without deviation, hesitation or repetition on one of the following topics: the importance of the title to our understanding of the novel; one character's journey through the novel; what they think is the climax of the novel; the significance of the setting of the novel; the importance of the first line of the novel; the importance of the last line of the novel.

• Have students make signs with the following words: language, structure, characterization, theme and context. Then have a student read out a sample essay and have the class raise the appropriate sign when they think the student has covered that topic in the essay.

Unit 4

Literary Heritage Prose and Contemporary Poetry

What you need to know

Unit 4 is assessed through a written exam, lasting a total of **1 hour 30 minutes**. It counts for 25% of the total GCSE mark and is split into Foundation and Higher tiers..

Unit 4 is divided into two areas of study:

- **Literary Heritage Prose (15%)**
  Students have a choice of two questions on each set text and will need to answer one of them. The first question will focus on a specific passage, while the second will refer to the text more generally and will require comment, criticism and analysis of aspects of the selected novel.

  Novels set for study are:

  - *Pride and Prejudice* by Jane Austen
  - *Silas Marner* by George Eliot
  - *Lord of the Flies* by William Golding
  - *The Withered Arm and Other Wessex Tales* by Thomas Hardy
  - *Animal Farm* by George Orwell
  - *The Strange Case of Dr Jekyll and Mr Hyde* by Robert Louis Stevenson

- **Contemporary Poetry (10%)**
  Students answer **one** question in this section. They can choose to answer a question either on one of the six set contemporary poets or on a single unseen poem that they have not previously studied.

  If they choose to answer a question on a set poet, they will have a choice of three questions:
  - A question focusing on a poem printed on their examination paper.
  - Two questions asking students to comment, criticize and analyse one poem from the poet they have studied from a choice of two.

  Students study fifteen poems by ONE of the following poets: *Simon*

Armitage, Gillian Clarke, Wendy Cope, Carol Ann Duffy, Seamus Heaney, Benjamin Zephaniah. All poetry is included in the OCR Anthology, *Reflections*.

If students choose to study the unseen poem (which will be printed on the question paper), they will be asked to comment, criticize and analyse the poem, which they will not have previously studied.

Literary Heritage Prose: Context

Students will not be specifically assessed on their knowledge of the social, cultural and historical backgrounds of their texts (as in Unit 3). However, they should know enough about the historical background of their chosen text to make sense of it.

Assessment Objectives

The Assessment Objectives covered in this unit are:

AO1

Respond to texts critically and imaginatively; select and evaluate relevant textual detail to illustrate and support interpretations.

AO2

Explain how language, structure and form contribute to writers' presentation of ideas, themes and settings.

4.1 Passage-Based Questions

Assessment Objectives

AO1

- Respond to texts critically and imaginatively.
- Select and evaluate relevant textual detail to illustrate and support interpretations.

AO2

- Explain how language, structure and form contribute to writers' presentation of ideas, themes and settings.

Ideas for starters

- Students work in pairs and choose a character from their set text. They write an alliterative sentence describing the character, or an acrostic on the character's name.
- Students write a paragraph about an event in their day, in the first person. They re-write it in the third person and compare the effects.
- Students look at the first line of their set novel. They discuss in pairs or small groups how the line relates to the novel as a whole. If used as an introductory activity they could discuss what it suggests the novel will be about.
- Students complete a cloze exercise on a short passage from their set text. This could be on paper, with a box containing the missing words at the bottom, or an interactive exercise on computers. They discuss how they chose the missing words, then compare them with the original.

Selecting text detail

Key ideas

- Students answering the passage-based question should focus on the passage but also be able to demonstrate knowledge and understanding of the text as a whole. They should be able to select and use quotations from the passage effectively. (**Presentation 4.1.1** can be used to introduce students to passage-based questions.)

ACTIVITY 1

 tweakit

How does it work?

Students are asked to group quotations from *Pride and Prejudice* under two different thematic headings.

Try this!

Students work in pairs or small groups and re-write the passage as a play for radio. They will need to think about what the narrative says and where sound effects might be needed. What music would be suitable for the beginning and end of the piece? How would they show the two themes of marriage and family relationships in this genre?

Or this!

Students watch the relevant scene from the BBC's adaptation of *Pride and Prejudice* making notes of how the screenplay differs from the book and how the two themes are brought out.

ACTIVITY 2    **tweakit**

How does it work?

Students write two paragraphs about two themes from *Pride and Prejudice*, with textual evidence to support their ideas.

Try this!

Students work in pairs to design a multiple choice quiz, using quotations from the passage. They ask fellow students to look at a quotation and tick whether it applies to marriage, family relationships, both or neither. They must supply the answers as well. Students then exchange quizzes and see how well they score.

Or this!

Students divide into groups of five. Two pairs make teams and the fifth person is the judge. Each team takes it in turn to call a quotation and the other team has to identify it as belonging to one theme, both themes, or neither. The judge awards marks. (They could be provided with a checklist first.) A strict time limit of five or ten minutes will help students to focus!

Evaluating your quotations

Key ideas

• When including quotations, students need to explain not only what they say but what they suggest. This can include references to overall themes and symbols in the novel.

ACTIVITY 3    **tweakit**

How does it work?

Students choose quotations from *Silas Marner* from a list and put them into a grid (**Activity Sheet 4.1.1**) to explain their direct and implied meanings. They write a paragraph relating each of the chosen quotations to the given themes and symbols in the novel.

Try this!

Students use the list of quotations to create a set of PowerPoint slides. Each slide should have a heading which is the quotation, an image related to the themes and symbols and a thought bubble which explains the implied meaning.

Or this!

Students use the passage as the basis for a graphic version of the scene. The quotations should be used as captions, the images drawn following the descriptions, and a thought bubble in each picture should give the implied meaning.

Interpreting a narrator's viewpoint

Key ideas

- The narrator's viewpoint is the perspective from which a story is told.
- A first-person narrative uses the pronoun I; a third-person narrative uses the pronouns he/she/they and allows the narrator to be omniscient.

ACTIVITY 4  tweakit

How does it work?

The students select verbs and phrases from *Silas Marner* to demonstrate how an author shows viewpoint.

Try this!

Students work in pairs to prepare online interviews with the two characters, talking about the events in the passages given. They take it in turns to be the interviewer and a character from the novel. (You could prepare question prompts if required.)

ACTIVITY 5  tweakit

How does it work?

Students are expected to write a short explanation of George Eliot's techniques in showing different viewpoints in *Silas Marner*.

Try this!

Students work in pairs to re-write each of the two passages as a soliloquy in a stage version or as a voice-over in a TV production of the book. They should add stage directions or actions, camera angles and a storyboard as appropriate. They could also suggest appropriate music as background for either medium.

Interpreting an author's use of language

Key ideas

- A good writer varies his or her language to create particular effects, using description, dialogue and narration.

ACTIVITY 6
 **tweakit**

How does it work?
Students work in pairs to answer a set of comprehension questions on a passage from *Animal Farm*.

Try this!
Students re-write the passage from the point of view of one of the animals, other than Napoleon and the dogs, using the questions as prompts.

ACTIVITY 7
 **tweakit**

How does it work?
Students are guided to write a paragraph about George Orwell's use of different aspects of language in *Animal Farm*.

Try this!
Students work in pairs to replace the following words with their opposites and discuss how it changes the mood and feeling: *silent, terrified, crept, bounding, huge, fierce-looking, wolves.*

How language supports ideas, themes and settings

Key ideas
- How authors write is as important as what they write.
- Authors use words, phrases and sentences to create effects that engage the reader.
- Authors also use dialogue as a way to support the ideas, themes and setting of a text.

ACTIVITY 8
 **tweakit**

How does it work?
Students highlight verbs and adjectives from *Lord of the Flies* to emphasize differences between action and description in writing. (**Activity 4.1.2** can be used here.)

Try this!
Students write two paragraphs, one about an active event, such as a fight, a race, a rescue or a crash; the other describing a deserted place or a scene. They work in pairs to read each other's work and discuss how they achieved their effects.

Or this! (for lower ability)
Display two lists of words on the board – one containing active verbs, the other descriptive adjectives. Students discuss briefly what types of words are in each list. They then incorporate some of the words from each list into two paragraphs – one active and one descriptive.

ACTIVITY 9

 tweakit

How does it work?

Students complete a grid (**Activity Sheet 4.1.3**) relating words and phrases from *Lord of the Flies* to ideas, themes and setting.

Try this!

Students use the two extracts as the basis for two scenes from a new screenplay of the book. Write the actions, sounds and camera angles and suggest suitable background music for each one. These can be storyboarded.

Or this! (to stretch and challenge students)

Use the two extracts as the stimuli for a pair of haiku, each with a different mood and tone.

ACTIVITY 10

 tweakit

How does it work?

Students use a spider diagram of ideas, themes, and setting, to add appropriate quotations from a passage of dialogue from *Lord of the Flies*.

Try this! (for lower ability)

Students complete their spider diagram individually or in pairs, using **Activity Sheet 4.1.4**, which gives them some help in completing the task.

Or this!

Students re-write the passage as an extract from the diaries of each of the three boys. Each one will have a different viewpoint on the conversation and its meaning.

ACTIVITY 11

 tweakit

How does it work?

Students use their completed spider diagram as a plan for a piece of writing on the writer's use of dialogue to support ideas, themes and setting.

Try this! (to stretch and challenge students)

Students work in threes, in role as the three characters in the passage. Each takes a turn at explaining how their character in the book and their dialogue in the passage relates to the ideas, themes and setting in the spider diagram.

Ideas for plenaries

• Finished spider diagrams or grids can be displayed around the classroom and students given five or ten minutes to go round and discuss or make notes from them.

- Students are given five minutes to compare the ideas they have used in an activity with a small group. They agree a common set of ideas. Each group appoints a spokesperson to feed back the ideas to the whole class.
- Quick fire quiz: Give out a sheet of paper with twenty statements about the set text. Students can circle the answer 'true' or 'false' and are given five minutes to complete the quiz. They swap papers and mark the answers.
- Students imagine one of the characters they have been studying has a Twitter account. They are allowed 140 characters to report their view of an event in the story.

4.2 Comment, Criticism and Analysis

Assessment Objectives

AO1

- Respond to texts critically and imaginatively.

- Select and evaluate relevant textual detail to illustrate and support interpretations.

AO2

- Explain how language, structure and form contribute to writers' presentation of ideas, themes and settings.

Ideas for starters

- Ask students to look at the following quotation and discuss the surface meaning and the implied meaning: 'I do not agree with what you are saying but I will defend to the death your right to say it.'
- Ask students to write a 50 word summary of the plot of their set text.
- Students work in pairs to cast the main characters of their set text for a new film or TV version. They should give reasons for their choices.
- Students find ten adjectives to describe the setting of their chosen book. They will need to justify their choices.

Interpreting an author's meaning

Key ideas

- When interpreting a text, students need to show understanding of both surface meaning and implied meaning.

ACTIVITY 1    tweakit

How does it work?

Students discuss a passage from the book looking at surface and implied meanings. They write a paragraph on the author's presentation of these.

Try this!

One student reads the dialogue from the passage aloud, pausing at the end of each sentence, while a second student utters the subtext (the person's thoughts). Students collaborate on writing two statements: the first beginning: 'I think the author's purpose in this passage is...' and the second beginning: 'I think this because...'

Interpreting an author's purpose

Key ideas

- The main theme or purpose of a story is the key message about life or society that the author is trying to send.
- Readers need to look for clues that reveal the author's purpose in the text.

ACTIVITY 2

 tweakit

How does it work?

Students complete a grid of events to show the author's purpose for each one, together with a supporting quotation.

Try this!

Students work in pairs to complete their grid, using **Activity Sheet 4.2.1**.

Or this!

Students work in small groups. Each group is given a theme or idea that relates to the author's purpose in writing the story. The group then designs a PowerPoint presentation where each slide shows an event in the story related to their theme, with a heading or a speech bubble containing a quotation as evidence. The slides may be pictures with caption headings, or words only, or a mixture of both.

ACTIVITY 3

 tweakit

How does it work?

Students write two paragraphs about what the author wants the reader to learn from the story, with suggestions given about specific themes.

Try this!

Students design a new cover for their set text, including a blurb and three 'quotations' from book reviewers for different newspapers which comment on what readers can learn from the book.

Identifying key events in the novel

Key ideas

- In order to explain the structure and form of a story, students should have a good overview of the whole text.
- A storyboard is a useful device for summarizing the plot.

ACTIVITY 4

 tweakit

How does it work?

Students design a storyboard to show the sequence of main events in their set text. They discuss what they have noticed about it.

Try this!

Print the storyboard worksheet (**Activity Sheet 4.2.2**) on to A3 paper and have students work on it in groups. The finished storyboards could be used for classroom display.

Or this! (for Speaking and Listening practice)

<u>Tableaux</u>: As an alternative to a storyboard, students compose a fixed number of key scenes from the novel as still tableaux. Each group can then show their set of tableaux to the class.

Or this!

Students work in pairs to draw a map of the island with the main features mentioned in the novel labelled clearly. They make a numbered list of the main events in the novel as a timed activity which is then compared with the teacher's list. Finally they use their list and put each number on the appropriate place on the map. They discuss the movement of events and what is interesting about it.

Analysing plot structure

Key ideas

- Most novels follow one of two plot structures: linear (where the story progresses in chronological order) or non-linear (where events are revealed through techniques such as flashbacks). (**Presentation 4.2.1** can be used to introduce this section.)

- Authors sometimes introduce parallels into their stories, where some events in the plot reflect others.

ACTIVITY 5  **tweakit**

How does it work?

Students look at two extracts from their set text taken from the beginning and the end. They discuss the parallels between them.

Try this!

Students use the two passages given as the basis for two scenes from a new animated film version of the book. They should storyboard their scenes, together with dialogue or voice-over as appropriate in speech bubbles. They should think about how they could bring out the parallels between the beginning and the ending of the story and choose suitable music to accompany each scene.

ACTIVITY 6  **tweakit**

How does it work?

Students put muddled events from the story in the correct order and decide what type of structure the novel has and what parallels are found between the beginning and the end.

Try this! (for lower ability)

Students can use **Interactive 4.2.1** to support them in sequencing events from the story. They should then work in pairs or small groups to decide on the structure of the novel.

Or this!
Students work in pairs to design a timeline for their set text. They mark the main events of the novel along this, giving the time span between each one. Students then work in pairs to decide how the structure of the novel should be represented as a diagram, for example: *a line, a circle, a triangle, parallel lines,* giving reasons for their choice.

ACTIVITY 7  **tweakit**

How does it work?
Students use the order of events to create a grid (**Activity Sheet 4.2.3**) relating cause to actions and events and relating these in turn to themes, ideas and setting.

Try this!
Students work in pairs to prepare a PowerPoint presentation showing how plot and structure relate to themes, ideas and setting. Each event has a slide which could include:
- a picture showing the event – or a summary of it in a shape box
- a heading giving the cause of the event
- three thought bubbles showing how the event relates to (a) ideas (b) themes and (c) setting.

ACTIVITY 8  **tweakit**

How does it work?
Students write a description of their novel's structure showing how it relates to the themes, ideas and setting.

Try this!
Students work in pairs. Each pair is given an event from the novel on a slip of paper. They then write a short presentation relating their event to the ideas, themes and setting of the novel. They present their ideas to the class as a talk, with visual aids, if they wish.

Interpreting an author's use of setting

Key ideas
- The setting of a novel includes place, time and situation.

ACTIVITY 9  **tweakit**

How does it work?
Students are given a collection of quotations related to setting and asked to put them into a grid to show what the author is saying about the effects of setting on characters and relationships. There is an extension writing task geared towards the author's technique.

Try this!

The grid can be completed using **Activity 4.2.4**.

Or this!

Students are asked to imagine that the Bennet girls have email facilities. They work in pairs to compose a series of emails that they might send to their aunt, and she to them, based on the information in the passage about Longbourn and its surroundings.

Ideas for plenaries

- Students work in pairs and select a character from their set text. They assume the character has a social networking profile (such as Facebook) and write a one or two sentence status update for the character which must reflect their personality. They feed these back to the class.

- Students are given prompt sheets to help them identify their own learning points in the lesson. They work in pairs to make brief notes to a time limit. They can then discuss their learning either in small groups or in a whole class group.

- The teacher displays two different critical viewpoints on the board about the set novel. Students work in pairs and write two sentences, one beginning: 'We agree with statement A/B because...' and one beginning: 'We disagree with statement B/A because...' They then feed their sentences back to the whole class.

- Students work in small groups to think of an alternative title and chapter headings for their set text, giving reasons for their choices. They have a time limit for this. They then send a spokesperson to discuss their choices with other groups.

Assessment Objectives

AO1

- Respond to texts critically and imaginatively.
- Select and evaluate relevant textual detail to illustrate and support interpretations.

AO2

- Explain how language, structure and form contribute to writers' presentation of ideas, themes and settings.

Ideas for starters

- Read a poem to the students a few times, then ask them to write down any phrases they remember. This makes a great basis for a fruitful discussion of why those phrases are memorable.
- Give students an image from a poem you are introducing to them and ask it as a riddle, for example: *'Why is water like green silk?'*
- Write the title of a poem on the board and ask students to predict what they think it is about.
- Give students a line from some poems previously studied from your set poet and see if they can guess the source poem.

Reading and responding to poetry

Key ideas

- Poets choose words to help the reader visualize the images they wish to convey and inspire thought about the ideas they raise.
- Responding to a poem is personal; not all readers will react in the same way.

ACTIVITY 1  tweakit

How does it work?

Students discuss their favourite film or music track to help them understand why opinions need to be backed up with evidence. It also makes a subtle link between poetry and pleasure. This would make a good starter.

Try this!

Students use the spider diagram on what to look for in a poem as a model to create their own spider diagram about films, music tracks, computer games, etc.

How poets choose words

Key ideas

• Students will be expected to comment on specific words the poet
uses.

• Connotations are the extra associations specific words have.

ACTIVITY 2

How does it work?

Students experiment as poets by completing the gap fill exercise on
Seamus Heaney's 'Blackberry Picking' and the associated discussion
tasks. They can either do this as a written exercise (**Activity Sheet
4.3.1**) or as an interactive one (**Interactive 4.3.1**). The full text
appears on **Activity Sheet 4.3.2**.

Try this!

Students go on to do the same with the second stanza.

Or this! (to stretch and challenge students)

Give students a full version of the second stanza and let them try to
make their own text by deleting words from it.

Understanding imagery

Key ideas

• We all use metaphors in day-to-day language.

• Poets often make up their own images, allowing them to convey
their feelings in a way that is both individual and precise.

ACTIVITY 3

How does it work?

Students read Gillian Clarke's 'My Box' and perform a guided
annotation. This will help them to access the metaphorical levels of
the poem. (Note: There is no *one* answer. The box may be her heart,
her memory, her mind. Encourage students to think of their own
hypothesis and support it.)

Try this!

Students can complete this activity using **Activity Sheet 4.3.3**.

Or this!

Students create a poster of the poem, using their own visual graphics
for what the box represents.

ACTIVITY 4

How does it work?

Students write their own poem using Clarke's as a model, helping
them gain an understanding of the structure and form of the poem.
For best results, guide them through the activity, sharing as they go.

Have a go yourself, to start the sharing off, so students will feel they can share as well.

Try this!

Students read out their finished poems to the class, and make a poster of their poem for a class display, around a copy of Gillian Clarke's. If the students seem keen to share more widely, set up an open mic session in a communal space at lunchtime.

Reading the clues

Key ideas

• Poets leave clues and ideas for their readers, allowing them to build up their own pictures.

ACTIVITY 5

 **tweakit**

How does it work?

Students discuss in pairs what they have in their schoolbags that gives information about them. This leads into a discussion about the character in the poem. This is a good starter.

Try this!

Students write a poem or short report about what their partner carries with them, imagining that the person has been found with memory loss.

ACTIVITY 6

 **tweakit**

How does it work?

Students are given a set of quotations from Simon Armitage's 'About His Person' and use them to write a brief description of their owner.

Try this!

Encourage students to use the spider diagram on page 133 to structure their thoughts. They can either do this as a written exercise (**Activity Sheet 4.3.4**) or as an interactive one (**Interactive 4.3.2**). The full text appears on **Activity Sheet 4.3.5**.

ACTIVITY 7

 **tweakit**

How does it work?

Students perform a guided annotation on 'About His Person' by Simon Armitage to help them discover the techniques Armitage uses.

Try this!

Divide the tasks between groups and ask each group to add their annotations to a copy of the poem on the whiteboard, or an enlarged copy of the poem for display.

Interpreting the poet's subject matter: experiences of school

Key ideas

• School is an experience shared by most people. Carol Ann Duffy explores this theme in some of her poetry.

ACTIVITY 8

 **tweakit**

How does it work?

Students work through the tasks with a partner or in small groups to arrive at some helpful annotations for each stanza of Carol Ann Duffy's 'In Mrs Tilscher's Class'.

Try this! (for mixed ability groups)

Give each group a stanza to practise writing a response to, using the questions as prompts. Piece it all together to create a good student response which the class can mark and grade.

ACTIVITY 9

 **tweakit**

How does it work?

Students look at 'The Good Teachers' by Carol Ann Duffy and answer questions on it.

Try this! (for mixed ability groups)

Using the words which indicate rebellion, students write a reference or report for the student in Duffy's poem.

Parody

Key ideas

• A parody is a humorous imitation of the style of someone or something.

• Some poets use parody to write new poems in which the originals are still recognizable.

Who is Strugnell?

Key ideas

• Wendy Cope uses a character called James Strugnell as a narrator in her series of 'Strugnell' sonnets.

ACTIVITY 10

 **tweakit**

How does it work?

Students discover what parody is by comparing Wendy Cope's 'From Strugnell's Sonnets (iv)' with Shakespeare's original and tracking changes.

Try this!

Jigsaw it!: Give students the original sonnet and the changes made to see if they can put Cope's phrases where she did. (**Activity Sheet 4.3.6** allows students to look at the two poems side by side.)

Or this! (for lower ability)

Working in pairs, students create further parodies of 'Twinkle Twinkle Little Star' and share these with the class.

Ideas for plenaries

- Students offer their favourite line from the poem studied and explain why they like it.
- Students write a prose version of the poem studied.
- Students produce newspaper headlines which sum up the poem studied.
- Students write a postcard to the poet responding to their poem, asking a question or expressing an opinion. These could be shared as a starter in the next lesson.

Assessment Objectives

AO1

- Respond to texts critically and imaginatively.
- Select and evaluate relevant textual detail to illustrate and support interpretations.

AO2

- Explain how language, structure and form contribute to writers' presentation of ideas, themes and settings.

Ideas for starters

- Remind students what onomatopoeia is, and give them five minutes to come up with as many examples as they can. (This is a good way to introduce Heaney's poem 'Death of a Naturalist'.)
- Give students an image from one of the poems they are to study. Ask if it is positive or negative, then ask them to change it to the opposite. For example, Clarke's 'long green silk' for water could be changed to 'slimy chains'.
- For poems with a persona, read the first line aloud and ask students to guess the persona. Release further lines until someone guesses.
- Ask students to jot down as many other ways of saying 'good' about a poem as they can in five minutes. Here's a few to start them off: *excellent, fascinating, interesting, moving, funny*, etc.

Themes in poetry

Key ideas

- Poetry is often used to express abstract ideas and often includes a wider theme behind the subject.

ACTIVITY 1

 tweakit

How does it work?

Students match quotations from Anthology poems to possible themes. Quotations are drawn from all the set poets, so this exercise is relevant to all classes.

Try this!

Using the quotation from their chosen poet, students see if any of the other poems selected could link in terms of themes.

Or this!

Students complete the activity using the drag and drop activity in **Interactive 4.4.1**.

Using poetry to protest

Key ideas

- Poetry can be a good way for poets to express protest.
- Repetition of strong consonants like p, d and b can be used to lend weight to an argument.
- In 'Bought and Sold', Benjamin Zephaniah criticizes how writers' voices may be restrained by the lure of fame. In 'Having a Word', he questions the jargon associated with politics, society and human rights.

ACTIVITY 2    tweakit

How does it work?

Students work through the guided annotation tasks to arrive at useful notes which lead them to understand Zephaniah's sound patterning in 'Bought and Sold'.

Try this!

Once the tasks have been completed, students read the poem aloud stressing the patterns they have discovered. This will lead to an understanding of how effective the sound is in making an impact in performance.

ACTIVITY 3    tweakit

How does it work?

Students learn about Zephaniah's lexical choices in 'Having a Word' and 'Chant of a Homesick Nigga' by completing the guided tasks.

Try this!

Complete Activity 3a using the linking lines activity in **Interactive 4.4.2**.

Or this!

For all of Zephaniah's poems in the Anthology, list the Black English words, the Latinate words and the everyday words, to conduct a lexical analysis of the characteristics of his work. Which words predominate or is there a balance?

Or this! (for higher ability)

Investigate some other poets who use Black English and see how they compare to Zephaniah. For example: John Agard, James Berry, Val Bloom, Grace Nichols, John Lyons.

Reading between the lines

Key ideas

- A villanelle is a poetic form characterized by the repetition of lines which occur at the end of alternate stanzas and at the end of the poem.
- Wendy Cope uses the villanelle to poke fun at lonely hearts advertisements and books from reading schemes in 'Lonely Hearts' and 'Reading Scheme' respectively.

ACTIVITY 4

How does it work?

Students explore the implied meanings in Wendy Cope's poem 'Reading Scheme' through guided annotation and then write a headline for a gossip magazine based on the poem.

Try this!

Students work individually to complete the exercise (**Activity Sheet 4.4.1**) and then compare outcomes with a partner. The gossip magazine headlines can be shared and enjoyed as a class.

Or this! (for higher ability)

Students produce a paragraph explaining how Cope makes the reader smirk in this poem, using brief quotations as evidence.

ACTIVITY 5

How does it work?

Students use the gap fill exercise to practise writing about Cope's poem 'Lonely Hearts', and then extend their ideas by writing a sentence or two on Cope's choice of form, in this case villanelles.

Try this!

Students can complete the activity using **Interactive 4.4.3**, either in pairs (if computers are available) or as a whole class using the IWB.

Or this! (for mixed ability groups)

Working in groups, students come up with an extended paragraph. The written paragraphs can be swapped between groups and peer marked using GCSE criteria from the mark scheme.

Writing with a persona

Key ideas

- Some poets take on a persona, so the 'I' in a poem may not be the poet (for example, Carol Ann Duffy takes on different roles in 'Stealing' and 'Mrs Lazarus').

ACTIVITY 6    tweakit

How does it work?
Students look at Carol Ann Duffy's 'Stealing' and answer questions on the effects created by the poet.

Try this!
Students work through the tasks in small groups and then feed back to the class.

Or this! (for lower ability)
Students complete the task using **Activity Sheet 4.4.2**, which provides scaffolding in the form of a PEE grid.

Or this!
Split the class into groups and give each group one of the four tasks to work on. (They are progressively more difficult.) The class then works as a unit to build up a total picture of the thief in the poem.

ACTIVITY 7    tweakit

How does it work?
Students read Carol Ann Duffy's poem 'Mrs Lazarus' and answer questions on it.

Try this!
Introduce the story of Lazarus using **Presentation 4.4.1**. Students then work through the tasks in small groups and feed back to the class. The first task is based on the first three stanzas; for the others students will need to read the entire poem.

Or this!
The first task could be used as a starter – a 'way in' to the poem. The remaining tasks guide the students through the poem.

Or this! (for lower ability)
Working as a class, make a storyboard for the poem, including captions, which then become quotations the students can use to write a response.

Or this!
In completing 7f (a role-play of conversations taking place after the events in the poem), students could use **Record & Playback 4.4.1** to record their responses. They can then replay the role-play and peer or self-review their work in role.

The theme of nature

Key ideas
• Nature is a common theme in poetry and has been explored by Heaney and Clarke.

ACTIVITY 8

How does it work?

Students read Gillian Clarke's poem 'Cold Knap Lake'. They first list the colours referred to and then look at how Clarke introduces the idea of danger.

Try this!

Students can complete 8a as part of their annotation of the poem. 8b is more challenging and can be used as the basis for a class discussion.

Or this!

Students can build on the task to compose a written response to the poem showing how Clarke creates a sense of danger and using the colours and other notes to support their ideas.

Or this! (for mixed ability groups)

The class works together with the teacher to write a response to the poem as above, but with the teacher modelling. Students continue independently once the first paragraph is completed. This could be extended into a homework task and selected responses read aloud as a starter to the next lesson.

ACTIVITY 9

How does it work?

Students read Seamus Heaney's 'Death of a Naturalist' and complete a set of tasks on the poem.

Try this!

The three tasks can be used to arrive at useful annotations and explorations, and can be done independently using **Activity Sheet 4.4.3** and then shared with the class. Students could then go on to draft a written response to the poem, using their notes and annotations and incorporating any conclusions drawn from the discussion.

Or this!

Students could use mind-maps to complete the tasks. For example:

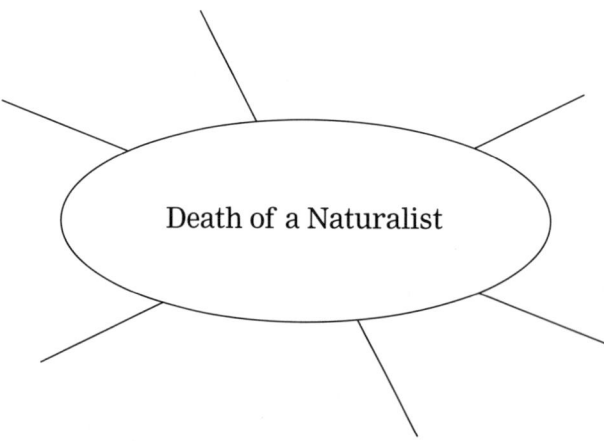

Poetry and the wider world

Key ideas

- Poets often have strong views about things happening in the world around them and use these for inspiration. (For example, Seamus Heaney wrote 'Punishment' about an ancient corpse dug up from a peat bog and Benjamin Zephaniah was inspired by the story of Stephen Lawrence to write 'What Stephen Lawrence Has Taught Us'.)

ACTIVITY 10

 tweakit

How does it work?

Students consider aspects of Seamus Heaney's 'Punishment' and then try to expand on a student response to the poem.

Try this!

Introduce background information to the poem using **Activity Sheet 4.4.4** and use this to start a discussion on what feelings Heaney creates in the poem. The discussion task leads into a writing practice task, using the example response on page 141.

Or this!

Display the example of the student's response on the board (**Presentation 4.4.2**) and ask your students to assess it. What is good about it? For example, clear points and brief quotations, etc. However, it does need to be developed. Where could it be improved? Give students ten minutes of silent writing time to work on it, then move them into groups to share and peer mark. The best example from each group should be read out to the class.

ACTIVITY 11

 tweakit

How does it work?

Students look at Benjamin Zephaniah's poem 'What Stephen Lawrence Has Taught Us', researching the background to the case and listing positive and negative outcomes.

Try this!

Set the Stephen Lawrence research as a homework task, then start the following lesson with a fact-sharing session. Students use their background knowledge of the Stephen Lawrence case to help with understanding this complex poem, listing positive and negative outcomes in a comparison chart. Train students to write 'Zephaniah's message' instead of the cliché 'what he is trying to say'!

Or this! (for lower ability)

Show students **Activity Sheet 4.4.5** and ask them to first look at it without writing any notes. They then have to jot down two facts they can recall, and share them until you are confident they have all the background knowledge they need.

Ideas for plenaries

- Give students a vague comment about a poem and ask them to improve on it. Comments from their own homework can be useful. Examples: 'it gives me a picture in my head', 'this is an effective image', 'the rhyme makes it flow', 'the rhythm makes it sound good'.
- When students are gearing up to write their exam, a useful plenary is ten minutes of silence to write about the poem they have studied in any given lesson, against the clock.
- Give the class quotations from the poems they have studied and see who can *Name That Poem!* This could be done in teams for an extra competitive edge.
- Vote a quote: from all the poems they have studied for Unit 4, what is their top quotation? Everyone in the class must contribute one. (These could be gathered on classroom posters.)

Assessment Objectives

AO1

- Respond to texts critically and imaginatively.
- Select and evaluate relevant textual detail to illustrate and support interpretations.

AO2

- Explain how language, structure and form contribute to writers' presentation of ideas, themes and settings.

Ideas for starters

- Give students a brief poem such as a haiku or a stanza from a longer poem to practise their skills on, such as the one by Angela Topping below. There are many good anthologies of short poems and haiku.

    > Who has dropped this purse
    > On the path spilling copper?
    > The horse chestnut tree.

- Give students a key term such as 'free verse' or 'simile' for the lesson, which they have to use either verbally or in writing during the course of the lesson. Make sure the poems you are using give them the opportunity to do this.
- For a homework task, students find a contemporary poem they like, using the library or Internet. Choose a different student each lesson to read their chosen poem to the class. These poems could be added to a display or a classroom anthology.
- Use the grid on page 146 to start off the lesson with a question. For example: 'I go flash, bang, thud: what am I?' (Answer: Onomatopoeia)

How to approach an unseen poem

Key ideas

- When answering the question on an unseen poem, students need to look at how language, structure and form support the meanings within the poem. (**Presentation 4.5.1** can be used to introduce this section.)
- Students need to back up their ideas and interpretations with close reference to the text.
- Students also need to think about why a poet has chosen to use a particular technique and how it influences the reader.

Practising annotation

Key ideas

- A good way to explore a poem is to annotate it. This allows students to record their immediate impressions and personal response.
- Students should add brief comments to the margins and question marks for parts they do not understand. They should circle words and imagery they find striking.
- Annotations may be made during the exam and will allow students to focus closely on the poem before they begin writing their response.

ACTIVITY 1

How does it work?

Students use the Angela Topping poem 'How to Capture a Poem' as a starting point to practise annotation. They then apply this knowledge to the un-annotated poem by Matt Simpson, using their notes to address the prompts.

Try this!

The class complete annotations on Topping's poem on the whiteboard. Students can then work independently on Simpson's poem.

Selecting quotations

Key ideas

- When writing about a poem, students need to provide evidence from the poem for their ideas.
- Short quotations as well as longer ones can be effective, and should include comment as well as the quotation itself.

ACTIVITY 2

How does it work?

Students read the response provided and discuss it, looking for strengths – things they can emulate, but also how they could continue it, using the bullet points as prompts.

Try this!

Give the response to students without the quotations, and ask them to find evidence for the point made before continuing it.

Free verse

Key ideas

- Free verse is a form of poetry which has no regular beat or set rhyme scheme.

- Free verse allows poets flexibility but still includes poetic devices.
- Free verse is well suited to conveying subtle and sombre tones because it is close to conversation in form.

ACTIVITY 3  tweakit

How does it work?
Students use the annotations in the book as a starting point for their own. They write a comment about how the assonance, consonance, alliteration, repetition and other sound patterns work together to create the music of the poem.

Try this!
Play students Chinese music, and then invite someone to read the poem aloud over the music. The rhythm and tone of the poem will be reflected in the music.

Or this! (for lower ability)
The poem follows the structure of a day in the life of this couple, beginning with breakfast and ending with evening. Ask students to create a cartoon strip with a frame per stanza, to fully understand this structure.

Or this! (for higher ability)
This is a love poem. How? Students will need to research the Chinese tradition for married women to wear their hair up.

Using literary terms

Key ideas
- Literary terms provide the vocabulary for commenting on language.

ACTIVITY 4  tweakit

How does it work?
Students match the literary terms with the correct columns of explanations, examples, effects.

Try this!
Students can complete this activity in three parts, using
Interactive 4.5.1.

Or this!
Give students the cut-up grid, and ask them to jigsaw it together and glue into their books. For less able students, give them the grid and ask them to find the correct term.

Poems to discuss

ACTIVITY 5  tweakit

How does it work?
Students discuss the two poems, annotate them and use the prompts to write a response.

Try this!

Half the class writes an examination practice essay for one poem, and the other half does this for the other poem. Choose some responses to look at after marking as an example of each grade, then set the poem students have not yet responded to for further examination practice. Assess their progress by comparing these with their previous essays.

Try This!

Teaching notes

- Activity 1: Put students into groups to ask them to invent their own definition on an A5 piece of card and illustrate it. Laminate the results and display around the classroom.

- Activity 2: This exercise makes the link between music and poetry very explicit. The last task could be a good homework assignment. The extension task needs a computer suite or should be a homework task. Any songs written by students could be recorded and added as a sound track to their films. Consider uploading the films to YouTube, to allow them to be shared easily. Watching the films in class makes an ideal starter and exposes students to poems in a very modern way.

Ideas for plenaries

- Have copies of single poems ready in the classroom in a special file students can access. Choose different students each lesson to take one, read it to the class and comment on it.

- Annotation is a creative act. Give students time to complete their own annotations using colours, highlighting, doodling, sketching, etc., then pair and share while you circulate around the classroom.

- Give students a framework for examination answers to the unseen poem. Have them write notes under those headings on some of the poems they study. Suggested framework: subject matter and themes; structure and form; imagery; sound patterns; personal response.

- Ask students to write a sentence about their favourite line from the poem, then read this aloud to the class. Collect in as students leave for a collage to put on the classroom wall before the next lesson.